The Basic Principles
of Effective Consulting

The Basic Principles of Effective Consulting

Linda K. Stroh
Homer H. Johnson
Loyola University Chicago

LEA
2006

LAWRENCE ERLBAUM ASSOCIATES, PUBLISHERS
Mahwah, New Jersey   London

Lawrence Erlbaum Associates, Inc., Publishers
10 Industrial Avenue
Mahwah, New Jersey 07430
www.erlbaum.com

Cover design by Kathryn Houghtaling Lacey

Library of Congress Cataloging-in-Publication Data

Stroh, Linda K.
The basic principles of effective consulting / Linda K. Stroh, Homer H. Johnson

    p. cm.

Includes bibliographical references and index.
ISBN 0-8058-5419-3 (cloth : alk. paper)
ISBN 0-8058-5420-7 (pbk. : alk. paper)

1. Business consultants. 2. Consultants. I Johnson, Homer H., 1935–
    II. Title
HD69.C6S77 2005
658.4'6—dc22   2005050733
                                               CIP

Books published by Lawrence Erlbaum Associates are printed on acid-free paper, and their bindings are chosen for strength and durability.

Printed in the United States of America
10 9 8 7 6 5 4 3 2 1

This book is dedicated to our families.

*We thank them for their love
and continual support of our careers.*

*Thanks to: Greg, Angie, Joe, Brad, Brandy,
and Brayden*

*Barbara, Jan, Jim, Rich, Linda, JD,
Jon, Joe Homer, Katelynn, Jill, and Nick*

Contents

Foreword

Robert L. Lorber
Internationally recognized consultant and author

This is the book!

If you check out the shelves of your local bookseller for books on consulting, you will find books on how to set up an independent consulting practice; how to market yourself as a consultant; and even how to make millions of dollars as a consultant. You might even find these books to be interesting reads, but my guess is, unlike *The Basic Principles of Effective Consulting*, you may never look at those books again. If you only read one book on consulting this year, read this one!

After almost 30 years as the CEO of the Lorber Kamai Consulting Group, I believe *The Basic Principles of Effective Consulting* is a book you will be drawn to repeatedly over your career in consulting. Just as Stroh and Johnson note throughout the book, when most consultants fail, it's because they have never learned (or have forgotten) the basics of doing consulting.

I had the unique the opportunity of writing *Putting The One Minute Manager To Work* with Ken Blanchard and *One Page Management* with Riaz Khadem; and "this is THE book!" It starts with Step #1 and describes the basics you need to become an effective consultant. Stroh and Johnson provide numerous hands-on examples of each step of the consulting process, from writing a proposal and securing a contract, to providing a feedback report, to initiating change in organizations.

They have called on experts in the field to write real life case examples relevant to each chapter's material. These expert cases exemplify the humanness of the consulting experience and provide advice from the pros in the consulting field (and those who are users of consultants). I had the great experience of working with one of these extraordinary contributors, Dick Bailey. Dick was one of the top senior executives at Kraft when he asked us to work with him and his team. As a leader, he knew how to work with, learn from, and manage large consulting projects. Read the chapter that includes the "From the Experts" section in which Bailey talks about "A Few Simple Steps to Implement Change." This is the type of quality content that can make a real difference for leaders, managers, and consultants.

The end of each chapter provides summaries that can be referred to throughout your career—summaries that remind even the seasoned consultant of how to remain successful in the business by providing checklists to ensure an effective engagement.

Moreover, the basic principles can be applied regardless of your specialty area. Whether it's information technology, or marketing, Six Sigma, engineering, or golf course design, the consulting model outlined in this book is outstanding—and it works!

Stroh and Johnson should be complimented on a job well done. In my 30 years as a consultant I only wish they would have written this book a long time ago. It could have simplified and made a huge difference to me and my organization.

I'm proud to introduce a book that will help each of the readers to improve the quality and effectiveness of the work that you do.

Enjoy the journey!

Preface:
Who Should Read This Book and Why

This book is written for novice consultants, project managers, staff advisors, and anyone who wants to learn (or be reminded of) the basic principles of effective consulting. The book is an introduction to consulting and provides a step-by-step process that nearly anyone can learn. Even a seasoned consultant would benefit from reviewing the material in this book. As noted in chapter 10 of this book, when consultants run into trouble, it is most often because they have forgotten, or have ignored, the basic principles of consulting. Although many people call themselves consultants, or operate in a consulting capacity, not all of them are able to successfully help organizations and their managers make their workplaces more effective and efficient places to work. With the onset of downsizing, rightsizing, and outsourcing, organizations call on consultants more and more to fill the gaps in their workforces, implement needed change in their organizations, and solve significant problems in their organizations. Regardless of the functional area in which you may consult, the key success factors and basic principles of effective consulting outlined in this book will help you become a better consultant.

The impetus for writing this book came from the many students and consultants whom we have trained over the years. They have told us that there are two important keys that are needed for training someone to be an effective consultant. The first is a general model of the consulting process—a step-by-step model that outlines the consulting process from start to finish. The second key is to have ample numbers of concrete cases and examples to explain what goes on in each step of the consulting process. A frequent complaint with other books on consulting is that they tell you what to do but don't show you how to do it.

We've used this feedback from consultants and our students to create what we think is a unique book on the basics of consulting. The book offers a step-by-step guide of the elements of successful consulting relevant to a variety of fields. We also provide numerous examples of real life cases. We tell our readers exactly what to say in the entry interview, how to write a proposal and a contract, how to do a diagnosis, and so on, and we provide many examples of how consultants handled difficult situations encountered each step of the way. We probably have more cases in this book than most other consulting books put together (probably a bit of an exaggeration!). Our students told us they want concrete examples of what to say and what to do, and that's just what we've provided in this book.

We have also added a set of key success factors at the end of each chapter. These success factors can be used in multiple ways. They can be used as a checklist to validate that you have covered the important steps related to each chapter's material (e.g., when writing a contract, you can refer to the success factors at the end of chapter 3 to be sure you have covered the important material in your contract or agreement). The key success factors could also be used in the classroom or in your company as guidelines for important topic-relevant discussions/dialogue. If using the book in the classroom, the success factors could also be turned into student projects.

In addition, we have added to each chapter "From the Experts" sections written by successful consultants and users of consultants' services. These experts share ideas and tips about their own consulting experiences that relate to some of the material discussed in the chapter. This feature of the book provides very valuable advice on how experts approach problems and challenges, as well as what worked for them and what didn't work for them. Again, as the consultants we have trained have asked, our attempt here is to provide the reader with some very practical advice on how best to deal with issues raised at each step of the consulting process.

We are hopeful that the reader, like the many consultants that we have trained, will find this approach valuable and that the insights that we have provided in the book will enhance your career success.

—*Linda K. Stroh*
Homer H. Johnson

ACKNOWLEDGMENTS

There are several people we need to thank who have made this book possible. First, we thank our families for their continual support and understanding. Next, we are thankful to Erica Fox for her excellent research and editing skills. This book could not have been written without Erica's interest and dedication to our work. Thanks, Erica.

We are also grateful to the experts who were willing to share their advice by writing cases for each chapter in this book: Amy Glynn, Dow Jones & Company Inc.; Maureen Ausura, Archer Daniels Midland; Kerry Weinger, Baker & McKenzie; Denny L. Brown, Linden Associates; Malou Roth, People First, Larry Anders, Anders & Associates and Sherry Camden-Anders, Alliant International University; Richard E. Bailey, Bailey Consulting; Elaine Patterson, Unocal Corporation; and Raj Tatta, PricewaterhouseCoopers.

Thanks also go to Loyola University Chicago, our colleagues who work there and the students from whom we learn so much. We would also like to especially thank the Organization Development graduate students who helped collect data and edited material for this book. Thanks, too, to Carmen Santiago for making our life easier in so many ways.

We want to acknowledge John Wiley & Sons, Inc. for permissions granted to reference material from the following articles below that were previously published in their consulting ANNUAL:

Johnson, H. H., & Smiles, S. (1998). Collaborative contracting: A key to consulting success. In the 1998 Annual: Volume 2, *Consulting* (pp. 285–302). San Francisco: Jossey-Bass/Pfeiffer.

Johnson, H. H., & Smiles, S. (1999). Gathering diagnostic information: What method do you use? In the 1999 Annual: Volume 2: *Consulting* (pp. 89–100). San Francisco: Jossey- Bass/Pfeiffer.

Johnson, H. H., & Smiles, S. J. (2001). The feedback/assessment report: Moving the clients to action. In the 2001 Annual: Volume 2: *Consulting* (pp. 229–248). San Francisco: Jossey-Bass/Pfeiffer.

Finally, we thank Sara Scudder, Senior Book Production Editor for her creative eye and helpful guidance with the production of this manuscript. Thanks also to Anne Duffy, senior editor at Lawrence Erlbaum Associates, Inc., for her support, faith in us as authors, and friendship. Anne, you are just the best!

About the Authors

Linda K. Stroh is a Loyola University Faculty Scholar and Professor of Human Resources & Industrial Relations at the Graduate School of Business, Loyola University Chicago. Linda has consulted with over 40 *Fortune* 500 organizations regarding such issues as motivation, leadership, change management, problem solving, strategic planning, diversity, international assignments and cross-cultural management. Dr. Stroh received her PhD from Northwestern University in Human Development. She also has a postdoctoral degree in organization behavior from Northwestern's Kellogg Graduate School of Management. She earned her BA from McGill University in Montreal, Quebec, Canada, and her MA from Concordia University, also in Montreal.

Linda has taught and published more than 100 articles, books and technical reports on issues related to domestic and international organizational behavior issues. Her work can be found in journals such as *Strategic Management Journal, Journal of Applied Psychology, Personnel Psychology, Academy of Management Journal, Journal of Vocational Behavior, International Journal of Human Resource Management, Journal of Organizational Behavior, Journal of Management Education, Sloan Management Review, Human Resource Management Journal, Journal of World Business,* and various other journals. In addition to this book, Dr. Stroh is co-author of two other books: *Globalizing People Through International Assignments* and *Organizational Behavior: A Management Challenge* (both published by Lawrence Erlbaum Associates).

Dr. Stroh was honored at the 2000 Academy of Management Meeting with the Sage publications research scholar award. She is a past chair of the Careers Division of the Academy. She was also named the Graduate Faculty Member of the Year at Loyola University Chicago (2000) and was selected as a Loyola University Faculty Scholar in 2001. The *Wall Street*

Journal, the *New York Times,* the *Washington Post,* the *Chicago Tribune, Fortune, Newsweek, U.S. News and World Report* and *Business Week,* as well as various other news and popular press outlets have cited Dr. Stroh's work. Her research has also been featured several times on *Tom Brokaw's Nightly News* and *CNN.*

In addition to her teaching and research, Dr. Stroh serves as the academic adviser for the International Personnel Association (an association of 60 of the top 100 multinational companies in the United States and Canada). Linda currently serves on the editorial review board for the *Journal of Applied Psychology, Journal of World Business,* and the *Journal of Vocational Behavior.*

Linda and her husband, Greg, have married children; Angie and Joe Gittleman and Brad and Brandy Stroh. They also just had their first grandchild, Brayden Gregory Stroh.

Homer H. Johnson, PhD, is a professor in the Graduate School of Business at Loyola University Chicago. He formerly was the director of the Center for Organization Development, as well as the Institute for Human Resources and Industrial Relations at Loyola University. Homer received his undergraduate degree in psychology from Knox College. His PhD is from the University of Illinois (Urbana), majoring in social/organizational psychology and measurement. As an active researcher, he is the author of some 80 articles and 2 books.

Over the past 20 years, Dr. Johnson has trained numerous consultants through his consulting courses at the university and his training workshops. He has authored several articles on consulting skills and is currently the consulting case editor for the *Organization Development Practitioner* as well as a member of the editorial board of that journal. He was recently awarded the Distinguished Contribution Award from Benedictine University, and the Lifetime Achievement Award from the Chicagoland Organization Development Network, for his work on change management and consulting.

An active consultant himself, Homer has provided consultation to numerous organizations, such as the Department of Defense, the Environmental Protection Agency, and the Social Security Administration. In the private sector, he has worked with Marriott Hotels, IBM, Safety-Kleen, and Alumax Mill Products. He has also been a consultant to the United Way, the National PTA, the Archdiocese of Chicago, and Loyola Medical Center, and other nonprofit service organizations.

As an active volunteer, he has been a community council president, the president of two local school councils, and directed the boards of two mental health agencies. He was the founding cochair of the Lincoln Award for Excellence in Education, which is the Illinois quality award for education.

He has been a very active supporter of his undergraduate alma mater, Knox College, which awarded him the Alumni Achievement Award in 2004.

Homer and his wife Barbara have two married children; Janice and Jim Rashid and Rich and Linda Johnson, and six grandchildren: J.D., Jon, Joe, Katelynn, Jill, and Nick.

1

Consultants and Consulting

This is a very good time indeed for consultants. As corporations have been reorganizing and downsizing, merging and globalizing, the consulting business has been booming. During the 1990s, U.S. revenue from consulting increased by at least 10% each year and by as much as 20% to 30% in some of the larger firms. Unfortunately, the 2000 economic downturn reversed these trends, and most consulting firms experienced dramatic decreases in revenues and were forced to lay off many of their consulting and support staff. Nonetheless, by 2003, a resurgence occurred, and consulting again became a growth market as many corporations turned to consulting firms to meet internal needs. This resurgence continues today. The future looks bright for consultants, as projections suggest a steady growth in the demand for consultants ' services in the next decade.

This book is about what consultants do and how they do it—or, more precisely, what effective consultants do, because there is a big difference between being a consultant and being an effective consultant. In the chapters that follow you will be provided with a step-by-step process that can provide successful outcomes to both you and your clients. The chapters have plenty of examples and cases of the process used by effective consultants, as cases and examples are one of the best ways to learn the consulting business. Also provided as part of each chapter are short pieces of expert advice by established consultants and users of consulting services.

Before we start with the details of the consulting process, however, let's define some of the basic terms and approaches used in the consulting area. And what better way to begin than with a case: the case of UneekGraphix, a company that is starting to feel pain caused by a decline in revenues. You might ask yourself, as you read the case, what would you do if you were the consultant who was called in by UneekGraphix. How would you proceed to help this company with its most recent problem?

UneekGrafix is a small graphics company that was founded about 10 years ago by 3 graphic artists who met while they were working for a major advertising agency. UneekGrafix quickly established a reputation for its creative, often-offbeat designs for CDs, book covers, display advertising, exhibits, logos, and promotional items. In 10 years' time, the company acquired several major clients and increased its staff from the 3 founding employees to more than 80 designers and support staff. However, in the last 2 years the company lost three major clients and has had difficulty finding new business. As a consequence, revenues have declined. Last month, the company had the first layoff in its history. The top management at UneekGrafix is both concerned and perplexed—concerned about the decline in revenues and perplexed about what to do about it. As their president said, "There is something going on in the market that we don't understand, and we have to get a grasp on this quickly before we take another big hit in revenues."

The UneekGrafix scenario is not uncommon in a competitive business climate. A new company is started by some talented people, experiences fast growth with a very bright future, and suddenly hits a wall. Company officials cannot quite figure out what's wrong. What they are currently doing has been quite successful in the past, but it does not seem to be working now.

This would seem like an opportune time for UneekGrafix to turn to a consultant. They are having considerable difficulty in determining what is causing the downturn in revenues, and a consultant could bring a fresh perspective to the problem. The consultant might conduct a thorough diagnosis, both of UneekGrafix's internal operations and its customers and market. Perhaps the consultant would make some recommendations as to what the company needs to do to reverse the decline in revenues. Or, perhaps the consultant might help the management team at UneekGrafix take a good look what services and products are demanded by the market and compare that with what the company is providing, and then help the team decide what direction to go in the future.

This case is a good example of what consultants might be called on to do, as well as why their services are so valuable to the client. In the chapters that follow, we look at how consultants have assisted a variety of companies and agencies. For example, there is the case of a shoe manufacturer who was struggling with the decision as to whether to begin selling their shoes online, the case of the Department of Child and Family Services of a large state that "lost" children in its system and turned to consultants to help them design a system in which all children in their care were accounted for and monitored, the manufacturing company that wanted to introduce Six Sigma in its facilities around the world, and the case of the consultant who was conducting a management retreat with the executive group of a large medical center when a hidden agenda quickly emerged was not part of the retreat agenda.

This is what consultants do: help organizations and individuals that have a need. The big question is how to most effectively help the client, and that is what this book is all about. Many consultants are very effective and make important contributions to the success of the organizations for which they consult. These consultants assist businesses in a variety of ways, from solving staffing and management problems to introducing new technology and helping organizations weather all manner of external and internal changes. Other consultants, unfortunately, are less effective—and less successful. Often, this is because they simply never learned the basics of the consulting process. They merely assume that because they have expertise in some subject area that clients will be eager to follow their advice.

The ultimate goal of consulting is to increase an organizations' level of effectiveness. This requires considerable skill and understanding of the organization's people, problems, and culture, as well as a strong grasp of the best strategies for assisting organizations to change. The purpose of this book is to provide you with the basic skills and strategies you need to be an effective consultant. If you follow the step-by-step process outlined here, you will vastly increase your chances of achieving successful outcomes for you and your clients.

We will get back to UneekGrafix soon, but let's first clarify what is meant by the term *consulting*.

HOW WE DEFINE CONSULTING

In this book, a *consultant* is defined as someone who either advises a client—another person or an organization—on the desirability of taking some action, or who assists the client in making a decision and then assists the client in planning or implementing action as determined by the client. Several points are stated or implied by this definition:

First, a consultant works for other people (or organizations) called *clients*. These clients, or beneficiaries of the consultant's services, can be individuals, groups, or organizations.

Second, a consultant helps these clients achieve goals that the clients, not the consultant, identify. The point here is that the client usually decides what problems need attention or what initiatives need to be implemented, and the consultant is hired to address these.

Third, a consultant provides a specialized skill or expertise that the client, or client organization, is unable to provide on its own. For example, it is common for companies to hire a consultant to train employees in a new computer technology or to conduct a study on a topic in which the consultant, but no one in the hiring organization, has expertise.

Fourth, although consultants may influence decision making by virtue of their knowledge or expertise, consultants usually have little power or authority to make changes. A consultant may recommend changes, and even how to make them, but the client retains ultimate authority over whether and which changes to implement.

To apply this definition to the UneekGrafix scenario, if you were to consult to UneekGrafix, the company would be called the *client*. You would be working on the problem that the company identified, which in this case is the loss of revenues, although that might lead to looking at different areas of concern. What you would bring to UneekGrafix is probably some specialized expertise in strategic management, or market analysis, or some related area, which the company does not have, or at least does not have with the level of sophistication needed. Finally, you surely will be able to influence what decisions the top management team makes regarding their overall strategy based on your research and expertise. However, the final decisions on what to do and when to do it rests in the hands of Uneek-Grafix's management. Managers get paid to make and execute decisions, consultants do not.

TWO APPROACHES TO CONSULTING

Now that we have defined, in general terms, what consultants do, let's get a bit more specific. Not all consultants use the same approach to serve a client's need. Regardless of the goal of the projects, consultants typically will take one of two basic approaches when they work with clients. They will function as *experts* or as *facilitators*. Although most consultants position their services toward one approach or the other, effective consultants know how to modify their approach depending on the nature of the problem or project the client wants them to tackle. In other words, they function as a combination of expert and facilitator, refining their approach in response to the needs of their clients. That said, let's take a brief look at the differences in these two basic approaches to consulting.

Consultants as Experts

If you ask someone to tell you what a consultant does, most people would describe a consultant as someone who is "an expert" or who offers expert advice. Medical doctors are frequently used as examples. You explain your symptoms to a doctor, who in turn asks you a few important questions and then tells you what you need to do to get better. The process is typically fairly quick and simple, although not always painless.

The situation is not too different in the business context. Usually, a client brings a problem to a consultant, who then asks the client many questions. The consultant may gather a variety of diagnostic data related to the problem—by reviewing company records or market data, for example. The consultant may also interview a broad sample of people throughout the business. The consultant then analyzes the data, arrives at a diagnosis of the problem, and tells the client what the organization needs to do to improve or eliminate the problem. On occasion, a consultant will also assist in implementing the recommendations, thereby taking more of a facilitator role.

Let's go back to the case of UneekGrafix and look at how an expert consultant might approach the company's dilemma.

Once the top executives at UneekGrafix made a decision to seek the assistance of a consultant, they interviewed three consulting firms that specialized in market strategy or strategic planning. Each firm made a presentation to the executives at UneekGrafix and, on the basis of the presentation and interviews, the company chose a firm that had considerable expertise in the graphics industry.

After the consultants had a good understanding of what the company executives expected from them, the consultants first conduct interviews with company personnel. The purpose of the interviews was to identify the products and services offered by the company as well as to understand what the company saw as their primary customers and markets. The consultants then began a series of customer and market analyses. They interviewed current as well as former customers of UneekGrafix. They also talked with companies that had never used Uneek-Graphix to better understand how the company is perceived in the marketplace.

Another focus was on the company's competitors—what were they doing that was bringing them business? The consultants also conducted a very thorough market analyses. They were particularly interested in examining which products and services were increasing in use and which were declining. Also of interest was an understanding of what the market would look like in 5 years, particularly how technology was changing the need for products and services of the kind offered by UneekGrafix.

Having completed the analyses, the consulting firm presented their findings to the senior management team of the company, both in an oral presentation as well as a written report. The report also included several recommendations as to how the company might reverse the decline in revenues and begin again on the growth path.

As the UneekGrafix example demonstrates, the obvious advantage of employing experts as consultants is that they have knowledge that is not available in the client organization. As the business world becomes more complex, faster paced, and technical, experts can be an invaluable resource. The consultants hired by UneekGrafix had several special skills. One is that they had a good understanding as to what type of information to collect and how to collect it in order to make wise decisions about the future. Moreover, they were experts on the graphics field. They also had a good understanding of strategy—how to position a company such that the company might establish a competitive advantage over its competitors.

The managers at UneekGrafix were stuck and didn't know what to do about the decline in revenues, and the expert consultants gave them new insights about their business and offered several valuable recommendations on ways to restart the business. That is why consultants are so valuable.

As with any approach to consulting, there are some possible problems for those who use the expert approach. One potential concern from the client's perspective is that the expert may not fully appreciate the nature of the client's business and may recommend actions that cannot or do not address the problem the consultant was hired to solve. Alternatively, a client may end up with some wonderful recommendations but be unable to implement any of them because of the unique politics or culture of the company.

All too frequently, experts present clients with nicely bound reports that detail the results of an analysis of a problem together with recommendations the company might take to help it operate more efficiently or compete more effectively. The report may be right on target, but because the report was put together outside the organization and the key company executives did not participate in the analysis or decision-making process, they may not take the recommendations seriously. Executives are bombarded with reports of all types, and unless there is a strong insider championing the value of its recommendations, a consultant's report can become just another document that is filed away and never seen again.

Consultants as Facilitators

A basic assumption of the consultant-as-facilitator approach is that it will ultimately be up to the client to decide how to solve the problem the consultant was brought in to investigate or to implement the project on which the consultant was hired to work. The consultant's role is to assist the client in going through the steps necessary to solve the problem or conduct the project. The consultant does not tell the client what solution is best under the circumstances. Neither does the consultant implement changes or take actions. Instead, the focus is on assisting the client in defining the problem, analyzing the situation, evaluating possible solutions, and deciding on the best solution and the best way to implement the option chosen.

Let's go back to the UneekGrafix case look at how a consultant using the facilitator approach might have worked with the company.

In an effort to understand and reverse the downturn, the company decided to hire a consulting firm that specialized in collaborative strategic planning. After interviewing three firms, they hired one that came highly recommended by one of their suppliers. After discussing what the company expected from their firm, the consultants designed a planning process that would involve and engage many of the key personnel at UneekGrafix. Each week, for 10 weeks, 15 of the key design and support managers met to complete a step in this process and, between meetings, teams prepared for the next meeting. For example, in preparation for one meeting, the teams called on current and potential customers to ask them what they needed and wanted from the company. In preparation for another meeting, the teams collected information on their competitors, particularly those that were taking business away.

The role of the consultants was to help UneekGrafix design the planning process and act as facilitators at meetings. They did not collect information for the firm or recommend a business strategy—that was the job of the UneekGrafix managers. Yet this does not mean that the consultants were ineffective. Quite the contrary—because of the process designed by the consultants and their facilitation skills, at the end of the 10 weeks the 15 managers who had been meeting had developed a strategic plan for the firm that they felt confident would put them back on the road to growth and profitability.

One obvious advantage of the facilitator approach we have just outlined above is that the client is very involved both in analyzing the problem and deciding on a plan of action. As a result, the client is likely to have a strong sense of commitment to and ownership of whatever action the organization decides to take, increasing the probability that decisions will be implemented.

Another advantage of the approach is that the managers became very knowledgeable about their business and about their customers as well as their competitors. This knowledge should be very helpful in making future decisions.

However, problems can arise with the facilitator approach. One rather obvious problem can occur if the decision makers in the client organization do not have the knowledge or the time to make wise decisions. We rely heavily on experts in all aspects of our lives, from medical doctors, dentists, and lawyers, to computer gurus, architects, and building contractors, to name only a few. These experts provide critical services in areas in which our knowledge is inadequate. Similarly, there are times when expert opinion is desperately needed in specialized areas of business.

Another problem that can arise with the facilitator approach is that the client group may not be capable of making tough decisions. In many collaborative efforts, the aim is to accommodate all the participants' viewpoints and to keep peace in the company. As a consequence, although a consensus may be achieved, it may be at the cost of making the best decision. Ideally, a good facilitator/consultant will make sure that this does not happen; however, the danger that the group will arrive at a less-than-optimal decision is a very real one.

This book does not favor either the facilitator or the expert model. As the examples we have mentioned point out, both approaches have their advantages and disadvantages. The point being made here is that there are several ways to approach a client assignment. The key is to understand which approach best fits the situation and which one will be effective in moving the client forward. By the time you finish this book, you should be better equipped to make such an assessment.

INTERNAL VERSUS EXTERNAL CONSULTANTS

Most people think of consultants as being self-employed or being employed by a firm that provides consulting services. These *external* or *outside* consultants are not regular employees of the client's company but work with the client on a temporary assignment.

External consultants typically spend relatively short periods of time at client companies. They contract for a specific project, and once the job is finished they move on to another project, and often to another company. Of the people who call themselves consultants, the largest percentage falls into this category of externals.

Among these externals, quite a few are "Lone Rangers"—people who are self-employed, work alone, and operate out of home offices. However, by far the largest number of external consultants are employed by consulting firms. Many of these firms are quite small, with 5 to 20 consultants. Firm sizes vary considerably beyond that. Among the largest consulting companies, a few employ upwards of 10,000 consultants. Accenture, the largest consulting firm, at least in the management consulting field, has some 90,000 consultants on staff.

External consultants are an immensely varied lot, with an almost infinite variety of knowledge and skills. There are consultants who specialize in everything from store layouts to recycling, product packaging, parks and recreation, risk management, animal care, inventory control, reading programs, water pollution, and nuclear energy. There are consultants who will help you design a golf course, others who will help you select the proper grass and sand, and others who will advise you on how best to manage your golf tournaments. Name it, and you probably can find a consultant who specializes in it.

However, not all consultants are externals. Another sometimes-ignored group of consultants are those who work for a company, often as full-time employees, usually in staff positions. Most of these internal consultants are employed in medium-sized or large companies. Smaller companies—for instance, those with fewer than 200 employees—either do not have the need for internal consultants or simply cannot afford to maintain them on staff.

Although some internal consultants may have the term *consultant* in their title, such as *organizational development consultant*, many do not. Their business cards may describe them as human resources specialists, safety officers, quality coordinators, product engineers, training designers, master teachers, financial analysts, or use similar designations. Their major responsibility, however, is to provide consulting services to other people or units in their organizations. Based on the services they perform, they are clearly consultants as defined in this book.

Now that you know a little about the two major types of consultants, you're ready to learn some of the advantages of working as an external versus an internal consultant or of hiring one to work for you (see Table 1.1). One advantage of hiring externals is that they usually have worked with a lot of other companies and have direct experience with solving the problem or conducting the project the client is tackling. For example, if a client wants to install enterprise-wide software, such as SAP or PeopleSoft, hiring an external consultant who has overseen numerous installations would be a critical and necessary addition to the process, especially if the client has little or no experience with such projects.

Another reason to hire an external consultant is that this individual brings a fresh pair of eyes to a problem or project. Involving someone who can provide a new and objective perspective can be a tremendous boon to a project, as we found with the case of UneekGrafix.

Still another advantage of hiring an external consultant is that it may be more cost effective than maintaining a variety of experts on the payroll with expensive benefits and compensation. Most companies cannot afford the luxury of having a wide range of experts on the full-time staff. Renting experts only when they are needed is a great way to receive help in specified areas, for specified periods of time, without adding staff and costs to the company payroll.

Although these advantages may seem like reason enough to hire externals, bringing on internal consultants also has its benefits. One advantage is that they are always available, assuming that they are not involved in a

TABLE 1.1
Differences Between Internal and External Consultants

External Consultant	Internal Consultant
Lots of experience with other companies	Always available
Direct experience with similar problems	More familiar with organizational culture
Fresh perspective	Understands politics of getting things done
Cost effective	Must live with results

project for someone else in the company. In addition, they are generally more familiar than external consultants with the company's people and culture. Often, they better understand how things get done, including who really makes decisions and what to say and do when approaching these people. In addition, unlike external consultants, who come and go, internals have to live with the consequences of a project, which can be a strong incentive to be concerned with the outcomes. Amy Glynn, an internal consultant at Dow Jones & Company, Inc., notes in the following "From the Expert Box" the advantage of being an internal consultant is that you remain engaged in the real-time evolution of the organization. Amy claims that

---

From the Experts ...
The Internal Consultant's Role at Dow Jones & Company
by Amy Glynn, Global Consultant, Dow Jones & Company, Inc.

Over the past several decades, many organizations have realized great benefits from utilizing external consultants not only for strategic planning but for re-engineering core processes and administering various corporate functions. But, while this strategy was largely successful, managing these consultants and their resources was often cumbersome and time-consuming. Typically, an external adviser does not have an emotional attachment to a client organization or a long term interest in furthering the organization's mission. External consultants and their firms are driven by revenue and the ability to provide new products or services.

In reaction to these issues, over the past few years, companies created the role of internal consultant. While their responsibilities are similar to those of external consultants, a few aspects of the job make it distinct.

The role of the internal consultant can be viewed as "insourcing" of the duties that were historically entrusted to external consultants: strategy development, process redesign, and so forth. The internal consultant performs the same functions but is differentiated by his or her commitment to the organization and the focus on one client.

My role as an internal international human resources consultant is to serve as a project manager to ensure that Dow Jones meets a set of long-range goals. I provide cross-functional oversight for a variety of projects by coordinating corporate staff globally. This involves managing internal resources as well as employing external vendors and consultants on an as-needed basis. For example, we are currently working on a project to ensure that all our employment practices are compliant globally with both privacy and discrimination legislation. This requires that I manage the internal resources of local management, the legal department, and the local recruiting functions. The management of external resources includes both outside legal counsel and local recruiting firms.

The advantage of being an internal consultant is that you remain engaged in the real-time evolution of the organization. Not only do I know Dow Jones's culture of success but I am also part of that culture. This advantage can be a disadvantage in that sometimes the most creative solutions require a fresh perspective and the ability to take a risk in making a recommendation. Therefore, the role of change agent in an organization requires credibility to obtain support from senior management as well as objectivity to deliver progressive results.

she not only knows the Dow Jones's culture of success but that she is also part of that culture. According to Amy, this insider information sometimes gives her an advantage over an external consultant when attempting to impart change in her organization.

On the down side, some internal consultants complain that their recommendations are taken less seriously than those of externals, particularly by top management. Internals are usually in the midrange of the company hierarchy, most often in a staff unit (as opposed to an operations unit). Because of this positioning, units or individuals may think that they can accept or ignore the consultants' services or advice. In addition, top management may feel more comfortable dealing with an external consultant rather than sharing the company's problems (or hanging out its dirty laundry) to someone in a midlevel staff position.

By this time you may be wondering which is better—being an external consultant or an internal one (see Table 1.2). If you are an external consultant, you'll probably get to travel a lot, probably will get to work on a variety of different projects, and will learn about the insides of a lot of companies. Certainly you're not going to be bored, and you'll gain valuable experience. Another plus is that externals are generally paid more than internals, and sometimes they have the option to turn down projects on which they don't want to work.

For some people, the advantages of being an external consultant can also be disadvantages. Some externals complain about the constant travel and about having to be away from home for long stretches of time. There are also likely to be many 12-hr days. If you're out on your own, you'll need to do a lot of marketing to find business. And, of course, like anyone who is self-employed, the mortgage and health insurance bills

TABLE 1.2
Advantages and Disadvantages of Being an Internal Versus an External Consultant

Advantage/Disadvantage	Internal Consultant	External Consultant
Travel a lot		X
Regular paycheck	X	
Variety of projects		X
Have to live with results	X	
Taken into confidence		X
Less boring		X
Company-paid benefits	X	
Often taken less seriously	X	

keep coming in even if you aren't working. Being on the payroll of a large consulting company eliminates some of these disadvantages in that the large firms usually have a specialized staff to do the marketing and to acquire consulting contracts, and they also provide steady paychecks and benefits.

Internal consultants usually don't travel as much as externals, which gives them much more time to spend with their families and friends and to attend to home responsibilities. They receive regular paychecks, and their employer pays for health insurance and benefits and contributes to a retirement fund. For some internals, working with the same people again and again, particularly if they are enjoyable to work with, is rewarding. In the negative column, this usually means that their clients and projects are less varied than those of externals. Often, internals are assigned a project, or expected to learn a specific set of tasks, and that becomes their specialty or focus.

As with any such overview, there are many exceptions to the rules just mentioned. Some internal consultants travel a lot, for example, and some externals don't; and some internals take home healthy paychecks, while some externals have a tough time meeting the bills. The important point is that within the field of consulting a major distinction is made between internal and external consulting. Whether to hire an external or an internal consultant, or to become an internal or an external, is a matter deserving of serious thought and discussion. This book should expand your understanding of these questions.

ORGANIZATION OF THIS BOOK

Now that we have the basic definitions out of the way, we can begin the details of the consulting process. The last decade has been one of continual change in organizations, and along the way consultants and corporations have learned a lot about the conditions and situations that facilitate change as well as those that impede or derail the process. For example, goals that are vague and not quantifiable (not measurable) appear to be an invitation for disaster, so one critical task for the consultant is to assist the client in clarifying the goal and the measurable results necessary for a project to be deemed successful. Involving key personnel who will be affected by the change also greatly enhances success rates; these personnel can provide valuable input and, through their involvement, ideally become committed to ensuring the success of the project.

The goal of this book is to teach you the basics of what consultants and researchers have learned about how to be an effective consultant. By following the process we outline in this book, you should improve your chances of success tremendously. This process consists of seven steps that, when followed sequentially, give an order and logic to the consulting process:

1. Establishing expectations and goals (chap. 2)
2. Formalizing the agreement: Proposals and contracts (chap. 3)
3. Developing a project strategy: Diagnosis and data collection; interviewing (chaps. 4 and 5)
4. Preparing the feedback/assessment report: Moving the client to action (chap. 6)
5. Presenting the findings: Moving from diagnosis to commitment to action (chap. 7)
6. Initiating action (chap. 8)
7. Ending the project (chap. 9)

The length of time it takes to complete each of these steps varies widely depending on the project; a step may take an hour to complete, or it may take several months. However, completing each step is critical to the success of a project, and ignoring the sequence (e.g., implementing changes without diagnosing problems) often guarantees failure. Chapters 2 through 9 of this book discuss each of these steps in detail and demonstrate the step-by-step process effective consultants follow. We end this book with some final thoughts that outline four basic principles of effective consulting.

Many people who call themselves consultants are unfamiliar with the process outlined in this book. Yet whether a consulting project is a success or a failure depends largely on whether the consultant follows this process and understands the principles behind it.

The focus of this book is on how to complete a consulting project to your satisfaction and the satisfaction of the client. At the end of each chapter, we provide a set of key success factors to assist you in making your consulting experiences more effective. For those of you using this book in the classroom, these success factors can be used as a guide for classroom discussion or for potential student projects. For those of you using this book in your consulting business, you can use these success factors as a measure or checklist for your work. You might also use these factors for important dialogue with your clients and colleagues.

Each chapter includes a chapter-relevant expert advice box that contains consulting advice written by an expert in the field. These boxes address a specific topic related to the chapter material in which the box is embedded. These expert advice boxes are practical case examples of the expert's experience with consulting and bring the chapter material to life.

Finally, at the end of the book, we have provided an annotated bibliography of books on chapter topics.

So, now that we know a little about what consultants do and what you'll learn from this book, it's time to begin to develop the skills for success.

2

Establishing Expectations and Goals

The success or failure of a consulting project is often determined in large measure long before a contract is signed or anyone has agreed to work together. This is true whether the consultant and client have never met or if they have worked together on many projects. In either case, the first phase of a project—typically the first face-to-face meeting—is extremely important, as this is when the expectations and goals of the project are established. If the consultant and client have never worked together, then the first phase of the project is also when both parties assess whether they will be able to work together effectively and comfortably.

For your first meeting with a client or prospective client to be successful, it is essential that you come prepared. You need to know which questions you want to address, as well as how to respond to the client's questions. In this chapter we discuss the questions you and the client need to answer during the initial phase of a project as you are getting to know each other, discussing the project, and evaluating the pros and cons of proceeding.

The goals and tone of the first meeting or meetings between you and a client or prospective client are likely to be different depending on the circumstances that brought you together. We therefore begin with a brief discussion of the ways consultants and clients usually make contact.

MAKING CONTACT

There are several ways consultants and prospective clients make contact with one another. Some of the more common scenarios include the following:

- A consultant calls a prospective client to discover the services offered by the consultant, and the consultant's firm. The prospective client suggests a follow-up meeting.

15

- A company has a problem that it needs help in addressing or a project on which it needs help. The vice president of human resources has received the names of three external consultants who seem to be qualified to handle the project and asks each of them to visit the company for a meeting and to give a presentation.
- The general manager of a manufacturing facility is planning a major project and knows she will need considerable assistance. She contacts an internal consultant with whom she has worked in the past and asks the consultant to work on the project.
- A department manager meets an internal (or an external) consultant in the company cafeteria, hall, or a similar location and asks the consultant to come by his office, adding "I have a problem I want to discuss with you."
- A consultant receives a letter from a federal agency soliciting proposals for a project. Interested parties are given a number to call for further information.

If you and the client have never worked together, as in the first example, the client will inevitably want to learn about your background and qualifications and, if relevant, that of your consulting firm. You will probably meet several times to discuss how the client might use your services, your strengths and qualifications, and your general and consulting-related experience. The initial phase of your relationship may seem to drag on forever. The client may not have even decided for certain to go ahead with the project you are discussing. Talking about it with you may be part of the process of making this decision. Considerable time— months, perhaps—may elapse between your initial meeting and when you and the client actually start working together. Frustration tends to mount in such situations. You are likely to feel as if you are saying the same things to the same people over and over again, yet no decision or payment is forthcoming.

In contrast, as in the third scenario, you and the client may already have an established relationship and perhaps have worked together in the past. In this case, you will have to spend little or no time getting to know one another. Moreover, if you are an internal consultant, you are probably obligated to undertake assignments that are given to you, and many of the decisions about how to handle projects may have already been made. In this case, the efficient way to proceed would be to discuss the details of the project as soon as possible and, if necessary, begin to draw up and sign a letter of agreement.

Regardless of how initial contact is made, several important tasks need to be accomplished during the initial phase of the relationship between a consultant and a client. The remainder of this chapter focuses on these tasks.

OVERVIEW OF THE INITIAL PHASE

The overall goal in the initial phase of a project, whether you are an internal or an external consultant, is to learn in some detail about the problem facing the client or the project to be undertaken. If you are not familiar with the company for which the client works, you will also want to learn about the organization.

The initial discussion between you and a client is likely to focus on the following:

- What does the client say needs to be fixed or to be accomplished, and why? What specific outcomes are requested?
- What does the client want you to do? What is expected of you? What will be your roles and responsibilities on the project?
- What units will be involved in the project? How well are they operating currently? Who will be involved in the project? What kind of support can you expect from them?
- What is the status of the project? Is the project something the client is just thinking about doing, or is the client ready to proceed? Are other consultants being considered for this project? Who makes the final decision about whom to hire? When is the project supposed to begin? When does the project have to be completed?

At some time during the initial phase of a project, assuming there appears to be a good fit between your skills and the client's needs, you may want to discuss formalizing an agreement or a contract to work together. In the next chapter, we review the details of drawing up such an agreement.

Whether the initial phase of a project is brief or lengthy, and whether the client is an old friend or a new contact, covering the points outlined in this chapter is good practice. This will ensure that you understand what the client wants, help to prevent either you or the client from making unwarranted assumptions, and give you a chance to learn about the client and the unit with which you will be working, as well as give the client a chance to become more familiar with your background and work style.

FIRST MEETINGS

Typically, clients initiate first meetings, usually because the client's company wants to hire a consultant for help with a project or to resolve a problem. If you and a prospective client have not worked together before, the purpose of this meeting is usually simply to explore the possibility of working together. The focus is on finding out about each other and on determining whether there is a good fit between what the client wants and what you do.

Obviously, clients want to hire someone who is capable of solving their problems and carrying out their projects, so assessing your competency will be a major concern. In fact, the client's highest priority will most likely be determining whether you or the firm for which you work is qualified to handle the work. If you do not pass the competency test, your first meeting is likely to end rather quickly.

You will want to address several key issues in the first meeting as well. The first is what the client wants done. What is the problem that needs fixing, or what does the proposed project involve?

There is also the important issue of whether you feel competent to handle the project. Can you do a good job? Are the project demands reasonable? In addition, you will want to determine whether you will be able to work with the people involved.

In the "From the Expert" box in this chapter, Maureen Ausura, corporate vice president of human resources at Archer Daniels Midland Company (ADM), discusses the qualifications consultants must have to work for ADM. We note throughout this chapter the importance of understanding the organization's history and culture. Ausura agrees and claims that to work as a consultant at ADM, the consultant must be flexible and find solutions that are consistent with the ADM culture. For Ausura, understanding ADM's culture, history, and business philosophy is a must. The consultant must also exhibit high levels of customer service and a willingness to work with the ADM team.

ADDRESSING THE SPECIFICS

Having outlined some of the broad purposes of the initial meeting, we turn now to some of the specifics. Suppose, for example, that a prospective client calls an external consultant on the phone or asks an internal consultant to drop by her office. What does the consultant need to learn from the client, and what does the consultant want the client to learn?

In the following section we discuss the specific pieces of information each party will want to learn during the initial phase of the project, as well as ways to elicit the information. Bear in mind that these are only suggestions. You should develop your own set of questions and tailor them to each situation.

Defining the Problem

Assuming that the client has contacted you, the initial conversation, whether on the phone or in person, will typically start out with the client

From the Experts ...
**Criteria for Selecting Consultants at Archer Daniels Midland
by Maureen Ausura, Corporate Vice President, Human Resources,
Archer Daniels Midland Company**

In general, I use consultants on a project or ongoing basis when expertise or data are not readily available in house. I therefore view our consultants as an extension of the human resource staff.

When the decision is made that we need outside expertise, a request for a proposal is sent to consulting companies explaining our need. Responses are narrowed to three to five, and those groups are invited in to make a presentation. During that presentation, the firm is evaluated using the following criteria:

- The consultants must be recognized subject-matter experts. Because we are depending on them to provide resources we do not have, we do not have time for people to try out new practice areas on us.

- They must have prior experience working with large multinational manufacturing firms. The Internet is wonderful, but only a small percentage of our population uses a computer on a daily basis in their jobs. Consultants who work with professional staffing companies frequently come in with state-of-the-art technology that will not work in our environment. Language capabilities and cultural understanding of locations outside the United States are critical in most programs we undertake.

- They must be flexible and willing to find solutions to fit our culture, business practices, and employee population.

- They must be responsive and available to the team working on the project. I expect a high level of customer service and follow-through before, during, and after the completion of a project.

- We want to meet the team who will be working on the project, not just the sales people, and hear from them how work will progress and definite answers to questions or concerns.

- The consultants need to be somewhat familiar with our business, philosophy, and history before they try to sell us services. I met with one consultant who spent an hour trying to sell me a program that we had just implemented. When he set up the meeting, he was very vague about the purpose, and we both wasted precious time.

- The consultants need to know when to stop selling.

- They need to be cost competitive. Cost is an important consideration, but not the only one. We look for consultants who are willing to work with us to find ways to reduce and manage the costs. We are looking for value and a return on our investment.

telling you about the problem or project that he or she wants handled: "Hi, I'm Mary Smith from X company. We are the second largest manufacturer of gears in the United States. We need help with a problem we're having in our marketing and sales department. Mike Johnson gave me your name as someone who might be able to help us."

Some consultants would respond by giving Mary a rundown of their impressive client list, what wonderful consultants they are, and how they can solve almost any problem. We strongly recommend against such grandstanding. Listening, not telling, is one of the most valuable skills in the consultant's repertoire. Mary obviously wants to talk about the problem—this is why she contacted the consultant in the first place. A far better response would be to say something like "Thank you for calling me. It sounds like an interesting problem. Can you tell me more about it?"

In this case, it would be better if the consultant let Mary do the talking but helped her maintain her focus on the problem. At the same time, the consultant needs to be alert to vague descriptions of problems or projects; references to "motivational problems," "communication problems," or "change projects" can have different meanings depending on who is using the expression.

Regardless of the terms that are used, you and the client need to be sure that you have defined the problem or parameters of a project in the same way before you sign a contract. Your task is to probe for more detail as well as examples until you fully understand the nature of the problem or project in which you will be involved. Questions such as the following can be helpful in eliciting the detailed information you'll want and need:

- What do you mean when you say your company is having a motivational problem?
- Could you give me some examples of the problem?
- How long has this problem been going on?
- Who is affected by the problem?
- How has it affected the people in your organization?

One of the reasons to probe fairly deeply is that the presenting problem—the one the client identifies—may not be the real or underlying problem at all. That is, the client may say that the company is having a problem motivating its line workers but, deeper questioning, suggests that the underlying problem is actually a disagreement between the union and management over work rules. Only probing questions will get to the bottom of the problem and thus to the underlying issues.

A word of warning is in order here: Not all prospective clients will want to go into great detail about a project until they have a good idea that they want to work with you. Clients do not want to hang out dirty laundry, or divulge trade secrets, to someone who may not be interested in the project or qualified to help them. Respect the client's wishes and do not push for details beyond the point where the client is willing to go.

The questions you ask will vary, of course, depending on the problem or project being discussed. The point is that your goal is to understand the problem or project at a fairly concrete and specific level. If you keep that goal in mind, questions should flow easily.

Agreeing on Expected or Hoped-For Outcomes

For a project to be a success, both you and the client need to agree on the specific outcomes for which the client is hoping. Does the client want a certain percentage increase in the number of employees who can use new software? Does the client want an increase in sales figures? If so, how much of an increase? Does the client expect the company's overall profits to go up? By how much? How the client answers these questions can mean the difference between accepting a project that is doomed to failure from the beginning and embarking on one that has a reasonable chance of success.

Among the questions you will need to ask is "Why do you want to undertake this project?" and "What outcomes are you looking for?" The answers should help clarify the reasons the client called you in as well as the outcome the client (or, equally likely, the client's boss) expects.

Addressing Past Successes and Failures

Sometimes it is useful to ask a prospective client whether the company (or unit) has tried to deal with the problem or undertake the project previously. In particular, you will want to try to find out if the client's company has tried to solve the problem with little or no success. Questions such as the following are good at eliciting this information:

- Is this a new problem?
- If not, how was the problem handled in the past?
- How have similar problems been handled?
- How successful were those efforts?
- Why were those efforts not more successful?

Plan of Action

It behooves you to clarify your role as soon as possible. For example, does the client want you only to implement action or to diagnose a problem and recommend a solution? You may want to ask the client directly: "Have you decided how you want the problem [or project] handled? Is this something you want me to help with?"

The work the client wants you to do will obviously be different depending on whether the client has already decided how to proceed. At one extreme is the client who simply wants the consultant to implement action, such as a training program to teach employees a new statistical process-control program. If you have the qualifications and are willing to design and implement the program, the project can move ahead quickly.

However, what happens if you are unconvinced that providing this type of training, or even training itself, will solve the company's problem? In this case, further discussion is definitely in order. It is often helpful under such circumstances to ignore the proposed solution for the moment and to reexamine the problem from a variety of viewpoints. When done diplomatically and sensitively, this approach often leads to a plan of action that better serves the client's needs and goals. This is one of the ways you can add value to the client organization.

At the other extreme from the client who has strong feelings on how a project should be handled is the one who has no idea how to deal with the problem or conduct the project; in fact, the client wants the consultant to answer this question.

Between these two extremes is the client who claims to be pretty sure what needs to be done, but, just to be sure, the client would like the consultant to come up with a diagnosis and solution. This situation frequently arises when there is disagreement among key players in the organization about how to proceed. The consultant has been brought in as a neutral third party.

Consultants who have faced this situation find three bits of advice extremely useful. First, you need to fully understand the dynamics of the situation. It is often useful to interview some of the key players in the organization to get their side of the story. Second, you need to remain neutral and objective. Third, you need to back up your conclusions with good, hard data.

Consultant's Role

Developing a clear understanding of your role is a primary objective during the initial phase of any consulting assignment. If you are not clear about your role after discussion of the preceding questions, you definitely need to clarify it. One approach is to ask "I think I understand your problem [or project]. What do you see as my role here? How can I best help you?"

You must understand, both broadly and specifically, what the client wants you to do. Only then can you decide whether you have the skills and the time to assist the client.

Sometimes clients are very vague about the role they envision for the consultant. In this case, you need to take a leadership role and recommend ways to proceed as well as outline ways you could assist the client.

Other clients have specific—sometimes very specific—ideas about what they want the consultant to do. They may go so far as to say something like "I need someone to facilitate the 2-day annual planning retreat for the company's management team on April 20 and 21."

Learning About the Company

The initial phase of a project is also when you should become familiar with the company or the unit requesting assistance. You might say, for example, "I think I have a good understanding of what you're looking for now. However, I'm not that familiar with your company [or unit]. Could you give me a brief overview?"

Clients usually are quite good at describing their companies. Occasionally, before beginning to answer, they will ask you what you would like to know. This is a legitimate question that you should be ready to answer. Most consultants start with the basics, such as the company's major products and services, and then ask the specifics, including some or all of the following:

- Who are the company's major clients?
- How many employees does the company have?
- Where are the facilities located?
- Where will the project under discussion take place?
- In a few words, how would you describe your company culture?

At this stage, you often need no more than a broad understanding of the setting in which the project will take place. However, depending on the depth of the conversation up to this point and the nature of the project, you may feel it is necessary to address a few specific issues, such as whether the employees with whom you will be working are unionized or whether the company is going through a downsizing.

Letting the Client Learn About You

Assuming that you and the client have not worked together before or are not familiar with each other, you may want to volunteer information about yourself or about your firm. There are a couple of ways to go about this. One is simply to say something like the following: "I'm sure you'd like to know a little about me [or my firm]. Let me give you a brief idea about who I am [or who we are] and the type of projects I [or we] have been involved in."

Alternatively, you may say something like this: "I've been asking you all sorts of questions about your company. I'm sure you have questions you'd like to ask me [or about my firm]. What would you like to know?"

It is good consulting practice to have a short presentation ready to introduce yourself—usually nothing elaborate or detailed. Here is one example:

I'm with a small firm of four consultants who have been in business since 1990 and have been quite successful. We specialize in the health care field and have worked with some leading hospitals in this area, such as County Central, Metro Normal, and Bethesda. Much of our work has focused on helping hospitals redesign their information systems to increase the effectiveness of health care delivery as well as to ensure compatibility with managed-care programs.

If the project under consideration is similar to other projects in which you (or the firm for which you work) have been involved, it is important to note this. The explanation might go something like this: "We just finished a project at County Central that was very similar to yours. It worked out quite well. Jim Haller was the person we worked with at County. You might want to give him a call."

Although the focus of this conversation is on selling your services, we recommend that you use an informational (and soft) approach. At the same time, you want to put your best foot forward. Everybody, even the most inexperienced consultants, has a best foot. Tell the client about your strengths and how they relate to the client's situation. No client wants to hire someone who lacks confidence and who is not good at what he or she does. So, although you should not lie about your skills or accomplishments, do not minimize your abilities or experience.

Prospective clients vary in how much they want to know about candidates for consulting projects. Surprisingly, many do not want to know much. They accept at face value that the consultant is qualified. In other cases, a prospective client may want detailed information, including people the client may contact for references.

In addition to a list of references, have a résumé available and/or an information packet about your firm. These can be sent to the client, or left with the client, to read when convenient.

Some consultants find it useful to describe their approach, especially if it is unusual. Details are not necessary; just provide enough basic information to highlight (and sell) areas in which you or the firm excel. For example, one human resource consulting firm prides itself on its collaborative relationships. Consultants with this firm typically form project teams consisting of 12 to 15 employees who represent a cross-section of levels and units of the client company. This team does most of the research and design concerning the company's new human resources policies and procedures, using the consultants as facilitators and resource people. The consultants with this firm claim that this approach leads to better policies and procedures as well as to greater employee acceptance of changes. Also, because they are proud of their success, consultants with this company are eager to explain their approach to potential clients.

Project Status

If the client has not been clear about when the project will start, it is a good idea to ask directly. The client may still be thinking about whether to do the project, or the client may not only have committed to doing it but also already has a budget in place. You can find out this information by asking something like this: "What is the current status of the project? Have you already decided definitely to do it, or are you still in the exploratory stage?"

Knowing the timeline for the project is also useful, if not essential. Asking when the client would like to start the project and when it will need to be completed are often important considerations in deciding how to plan your time and accommodate other commitments.

Hiring Issues

Many consultants suggest that at some point in the initial phase of a project that you find out from the client who will be doing the hiring. You might inquire, for example: "Who will be deciding which consultant gets this job? Will that be you, or will others be involved in the decision making?"

It may well be that the person with whom you have been meeting does not have final decision-making authority over which consultant gets the job. Or perhaps this person will make a recommendation and someone else will have the final say, or perhaps he or she was asked to find four or five consultants who seem able to handle the project and to submit their names to some other person or persons who will decide. Whatever the process, you need to focus much of your attention on the person who will be deciding whom to hire.

Fees

Most clients do not ask about fees during initial meetings. They have something that needs to be fixed or changed, and their focus is on finding someone capable of taking care of it. This is less true in the nonprofit sector. Because nonprofit firms often have very limited budgets, prospective clients with nonprofits may be quick to ask about your fees. If the client says there are limited funds for the project, assure the client that there might be ways to complete some or all of the project within the allocated budget.

As a general rule of thumb, if the client asks your fees, answer as honestly as possible. If you have a set daily fee, tell the client this figure. If you bill on a project basis, explain that it is impossible to quote a project fee until there are well-defined project parameters.

Commenting on the Competition

Clients sometimes ask consultants to compare themselves with the competition. This is always a difficult question to answer. Most consultants hear only bits and pieces about their competitors and rarely see them in action, so it is somewhat unfair even to ask a consultant to make a comparison. Some consultants note that they have limited information and therefore are not able to compare themselves with other individuals or firms. However, being able to benchmark your work and pricing is important to your consulting success. One way of better understanding your competition is to join professional organizations in your area of expertise. The associations often provide benchmarking studies to their members that can help with your pricing and projects.

Regardless of how much or how little information you have about your competition, never badmouth other consultants, as this reflects negatively on the whole profession. Instead, emphasize your ability to handle the project under discussion and focus on similar projects you have handled successfully.

If your style differs considerably from a competitor's, you may want to point this out. Consulting firms have different areas of specialization, and they differ in approach or strategy. Making clients aware of these differences assists them in making informed decision about whom to hire.

Discussing Bad Experiences

Occasionally, a client will say something like: "We have had bad experiences with consultants in the past. How do we know that working with you will be different?"

One effective way to handle this question is to ask the person about those experiences: "What happened? What should the consultant have done differently? What would have made the consulting process better?" Ideally, the consultant will then suggest ways to structure the project to ensure that the same problems do not occur.

Focus on talking about your credentials, as well as those of any other consultants who will be working with you. Also strive to shift the discussion to past successes in similar organizations or similar projects. Finally, you may want to explain that by working to develop a relationship characterized by collaboration and the client's involvement, you and the client should be able to significantly improve the chances of achieving positive results.

DECIDING WHETHER TO PROCEED

Consultants turn down projects for any number of reasons, including scheduling conflicts and concerns about the details of a project. To avoid wasting each other's time, you should let the client know as soon as possible if you will not be able to proceed. The direct approach—that is, telling the client directly that you are unable to do the project, and why—usually works best. Then send a follow-up letter to thank the client for setting up the meeting and to express interest in possibly working together in the future. You may want to recommend another consultant to handle the project, either during the meeting or in the thank-you note.

If you are interested in working on the project and eager to proceed, or at least to discuss the project further, make this clear. You might want to say something like this: "This sounds like a very interesting project. I've handled several projects like this successfully in the past and feel confident I could do a good job. How would you like to proceed?"

If you and the client have been discussing the project over the telephone or at an off-site location, you might suggest visiting the client for an hour or so at the client's place of business. This offers both of you a chance to continue talking and may give you an opportunity to talk to some of the other people who will be involved in the project, including key decision makers. This is good practice for both external consultants and internal consultants.

PREPARING FOR A VISIT

Before the visit, you may want to ask the client for printed information about the company, such as an annual report, information about the company's products, and perhaps an organizational chart. The Internet is also a good source of information about corporations. In addition to reviewing the company's Web site, you may want to search the online business press for newspaper and magazine articles on the company. Articles in the popular and business press can also yield valuable information on the company's market, whether it is a publicly held, and financial data. Coming prepared for an on-site meeting is critical.

Many consultants send a letter or an e-mail confirming the time and location of the meeting and to say that they are looking forward to getting together with the client and other key people in the company. They also include information about themselves and/or their firms. If you will be making a presentation, you may want to confirm the preferred content and length of the talk.

VISITING

The purpose of an on-site visit is to ensure that the right chemistry exists between you and the client. Making a positive impression is important. Managers as well as other employees are likely to be evaluating your interpersonal skills as well as your overall image. Dress professionally, and be sure to demonstrate your best skills interacting with others.

You typically will meet first with the contact person at the company, to review the agenda or itinerary. This provides a good opportunity for you to talk more about the project or issue with the client.

Frequently, you will be making a presentation before several people who will be involved in the project or for key decision makers in the company. Presentations are typically about 20 to 30 minutes long but may last up to an hour with questions. Plan on using overheads, PowerPoint slides, or other visual tools to highlight key points and to reinforce your message.

The presentation should be clear and free of jargon, well organized, and offer practical approaches and solutions. Corporate boardrooms are not the place to recycle a presentation you gave in college or a conference paper on recent theories in the field.

You will usually be asked to talk about how you would deal with the problem or project at hand. The presentation outline might be as follows:

- Thank everyone for the invitation to visit.
- Acknowledge the problem to be addressed or the project to be undertaken and review what the client would like to accomplish.
- Talk briefly about your experience or your firm's experience in dealing with such assignments.
- Briefly outline how you would approach the problem, while noting that you would need input from the client before deciding exactly how to proceed. Include examples of work you have done with other clients, particularly those in similar businesses. Also note how your choice of an approach would help the client accomplish its goals.

Be sure to allow plenty of time for discussion. This is essential. To get the discussion going, you might want to ask the members of the group for their reactions to the presentation. Questions such as "Is this the approach you are looking for?" and "What suggestions do you have for improving the method?" are appropriate.

Take advantage of the discussion period to gather information from the perspective of company personnel on the problem or project and, equally important, how the people think it should be handled.

Consultants often interview key people who will be involved in the decision about which consultant to hire or who is affected by the problem or project. Interviews can be brief —20 to 30 minutes each, enough to give each person time to offer his or her perspective. The questions you should ask should be similar to the ones discussed during the initial consultant-client meeting. (Of course, they will need to be modified to fit the situation.) For example, you should probably start by telling the person you are interviewing a little about yourself or the firm for which you work and what precipitated your visit to the company. You might then say something like this: "Mary has given me some background on the problem you're having in Marketing and Sales. I wonder if you could give me your perspective on the problem, especially how it's affecting your unit."

Next, you may want to explore how the person thinks the problem should be handled. You may also want to talk briefly about some of the specifics of your approach. At the conclusion of the interview, express your desire to work with the employee, and assure the person that the project will be handled as effectively as possible.

By this time, you should have plenty of information about the company and a good idea as to an approach to handling the company's project or solving its problem. You may well want to share some of these ideas and observations and to begin discussing how best to proceed. The client may want to go in to some detail about approaches the company has tried that have failed. The client may also want to go over some of the specifics of the project, such as when it will start, how long it will take, and important deadlines.

As we mentioned earlier, at some time in the initial interviews you need to find out who has final decision-making authority about which consultant to hire. It may well be that the person who initially contacted you has this power, or perhaps this person will recommend a consultant and someone else will have the final say. It may also be that your contact was asked to find four or five consultants who seem able to handle the project. The initial contact would then submit those names to some person or persons who will decide who gets the job. Whatever the process, you need to focus much of your attention on the decision makers.

Be sure to write a follow-up letter saying that you enjoyed visiting and that you would very much like to work with the client.

GAINING DECISION-MAKERS' TRUST

The next step is to ensure that the decision makers are comfortable working with you and serious about proceeding. The best way to make this happen and increase your odds of landing a contract is to be sure you have achieved everything you set out to accomplish during the initial phase of the project. These objectives can be summarized in the following questions:

- Do you have a good understanding of the client's problem or project?
- Do you have a good understanding of what the client wants you to do?
- Have you gathered enough information about the client's company—at least, enough to feel comfortable working with this client?
- Have you clearly explained your approach, including any unique features? Are you comfortable that the client appreciates and accepts your approach, including these features?

Assuming that you have decided that you want to work on this project, it is now time to get serious about getting a contract. We will discuss the details of contracts in the next chapter. For now, emphasize that you are interested in working on the project and confident you can do a good job. Saying something like the following is appropriate:

I think I have a good understanding of what you are looking for, and I am [or we are] very interested in working with you. I [or we] have been quite successful with projects like this in the past, and I think we can provide just what you're looking for on this project. I'd like to start putting together a project plan as well as a letter of agreement. Do you have any suggestions as to how we might proceed?

Alternatively, you might suggest a way to proceed:

I would like to start putting together a strategy and project plan as well as a letter of agreement. I'd like to sit down with you and any other key people either now or at another time and start outlining the details, such as when we can start, who should be involved, and so on. Does that sound like an acceptable strategy?

Sometimes the client will want to continue the discussion right then. At other times, the client will ask to first see a proposal, including a breakdown of costs. In either case, you and the client should spend some more time going over details of both the project and how to proceed. Having these details at hand will be useful when it comes time to writing the proposal.

In some cases, clients may say that they need to "check with some of the other managers" before proceeding or "think about the project before making a final decision." They may be interviewing other consultants and unable to make a decision about whom to hire until everyone has been interviewed.

Delays in making a decision about whom to hire are not uncommon. The client may have concerns about a consultant's qualifications or the fit between them that he or she may not have expressed. In an effort to determine whether there are nonverbalized issues about which the client is concerned, you may want to say something like "Do you have any concerns about anything I've said or about my [or our] approach?" This is a good time to deal with any concerns the client may have about the consultant's style or approach. If the client does not volunteer any specifics, then you may want to ask when you should be in touch.

SUMMARY

Before the consultant and client can sign a contract and develop a strategy for addressing a problem or project, there must be a consensus on the definition of the problem or nature of the project, what the client wants done, as well as whether there is a good fit between the client's needs and the consultant's capabilities. Failure to fully answer these questions before moving into the next stage of signing a contract and developing a project strategy is inviting disaster. Addressing these issues early in the project, before either party has made any commitment, is not only good consulting practice but also an effective way to increase the odds of successful outcomes.

Ensuring that you can answer each of the following key success factor questions is critical to having an effective first phase of a consulting project and later on as well.

KEY SUCCESS FACTOR FOR ESTABLISHING EXPECTATIONS AND GOALS

- Do you understand the client's project or problem?
- Do you understand why the client wants to undertake the project as well as the outcomes the client expects?
- Do you know what the client expects of you?
- Have you learned about the organization or unit requesting the services?

- Have you gathered as much information about the company culture as possible?
- Have you found out who the decisionmaker is for the project?
- Have you familiarized the client with your experience or the strengths of your firm and how you typically approach a problem?
- Have you decided whether you want to pursue the assignment? Do you have the interest, the time, and the skill to complete it effectively?
- If the project is one you want to undertake, have you committed to entering into a formal agreement with the client?

3

Formalizing the Agreement: Proposals and Contracts

By the time you have successfully completed the first phase of the consulting process, as outlined in chapter 2, you and the prospective client will probably have a good understanding of the purpose of the project as well as the desired outcomes. Moreover, you will probably have decided on a basic strategy for accomplishing those outcomes, as well as on your expectations and roles.

That's a great start! However, the project cannot begin until you and the prospective client formalize, in writing, the details of what you have decided.

Most often it is the consultant's responsibility to prepare this document and to submit it for approval to the client. The document may be in the form of a letter of agreement or a formal proposal (these terms are defined more clearly a bit later). If the client accepts the conditions of the letter of agreement or proposal as submitted or as amended, and if both parties acknowledge their desire to and, the conditions under which they will work together, then a legal agreement (contract) has been reached. To summarize, the proposal/contract phase of a consulting assignment starts with the preparation of a proposal or a letter of agreement and ends when both the consultant and the client sign an agreement to proceed with the project they have been discussing.

If you have ever purchased a car or a house or taken out a loan, you probably are well aware of the amount of paperwork that often accompanies these transactions. Although filling out reams of forms may be time consuming and a bit frustrating, it is an essential part of the process of making large purchases, as the forms detail in very specific language both parties' obligations and rights. That is exactly the purpose of the formal agreement that you and the prospective client will sign.

Up until this point, you and the client have probably talked about the project in only general terms. You have probably been focusing on trying to understand what the client wants to accomplish, and the client, in turn, may have been soliciting ideas from you on how best to meet the company's objectives. In this consulting phase, you and the client will work out and put in writing the project strategy, including what work will be done, where it will be done, who has responsibility for what, when the work will start and end, and the cost of the project. Ideally, during this phase, any problems that could hinder the success of the project will be identified, discussed, and resolved. Agreeing to, and committing the details and responsibilities of the project to writing, is one very important reason that the contracting phase is so critical to the success of any consulting project.

Another reason the contracting phase is critical is that this is when you and the client enter into a contract that will be in effect for the duration of the project. A contract is a legally binding agreement—in this case, between you and the client organization—that outlines your obligations and responsibilities and those of the client. Because both you and the client commit to whatever is stipulated in the agreement, it is important that considerable thought and care go into the preparation of this document.

This is not to say that all contracts are absolutely final and cannot be changed during the life of a project. Indeed, there is likely to be constant discussion and contracting between you and the client throughout the project. For example, the original contract may have stipulated that the staff at all five of the company's facilities would receive training in quality techniques; however, because the company has recently acquired three more sites, modification of the agreement is necessary. Or, perhaps two of the original sites were closed, or a new group of managers has taken over part way into the project and wants to shift the emphasis of the project. Any of these events may necessitate a change in plans and thus a change in the contract. As with the original document, however, both parties need to agree to any revisions.

Because so many companies and government agencies request proposals or letters of agreement before hiring a consultant, we devote much of this chapter to the preparation of these documents. Whether a proposal is detailed and well constructed or general and hastily written can mean the difference between whether the consultant who wrote the proposal is hired or the project is awarded to someone else. In other words, writing an effective proposal or letter of agreement is critical. Before going into the mechanics, however, we first need to define some of the frequently used terms and consider some legal issues of proposals and contracts.

CLARIFYING THE TERMS

The terms *proposal, letter of agreement,* and *contract* are often used quite loosely and can raise more questions than they answer. In the following sections, we sort out the differences among them.

Proposals

When an agency of the federal government is seeking help with a project, it issues a request for proposals (RFP). The RFP outlines the work the agency would like done and, sometimes, the type of firm it thinks would be qualified to do the work. Firms that want to bid on the work respond to the RFP by submitting a proposal to the agency. The proposal describes, among other things, how the firm would handle the project and how much it would charge to do the work. Sometimes the proposal also includes support materials that attest to the firm's capability to complete this type of project effectively.

The government agency that issued the RFP then reviews the proposals it has received and awards a contract to one of the firms. The firm that submitted the winning proposal is given a formal contract, drawn up by the government agency and the consulting firm. This is a legal document, binding on both parties, that describes in detail what the consulting firm will do as well as the payment it will receive. When both parties sign the agreement, it becomes a contract to which both sides must adhere.

Proposals are very common for government projects, and they also are used in the private sector. Most often, they are required by companies looking to initiate large-scale projects, for example, the installation of an enterprisewide software system. In this case, the company may solicit proposals from several consulting groups that specialize in such work, choose one, and draw up a formal contract between the company and the firm.

As the term suggests, proposals outline (or *propose*) how the consultant or consulting agency will perform the work the client desires. They usually include the various tasks to be completed, timelines, fees, the consultant's qualifications, and whatever other information the client has requested. This information may be presented in several formats—as a brief memo, a letter, or a lengthy formal document—depending on the client's specifications.

On occasion, a proposal is accepted as is by the client. At other times, the client will ask for changes to the proposal. Certainly another option is that the client will not accept the proposal and will award the contract to another consultant.

Contracts

The term *contract* usually refers to a legally binding document, often prepared with the help of an attorney. When signed by both the seller and buyer, for example, a real estate contract officially and legally turns over the ownership of a house from one owner to another.

In the example used earlier, the contract between the government agency and the consulting agency is usually drawn up with the help of an attorney and legally commits the consultant to do the desired work and commits the agency to pay the consultant.

A consulting contract typically will cover such matters as what work the consultant will perform and what the consultant will get paid. The contract may also cover a variety of other legal issues, such has who has the rights to material the consultant develops while under contract to the client and the conditions under which the contract may be terminated. The contract may even contain a noncompete clause restricting the consultant from working for one of the company's competitors within a designated time period. Both parties, the consultant and the client, must agree to all parts of the document and must sign the contract before it is legally binding and will be honored in a court of law.

There is considerable diversity of opinion as to the preferred form and length of proposals and even whether a written document is necessary unless a client specifically requests one. Always put the details of any assignment on which you will be working in writing, and have some written record that the client has agreed to the terms you have laid out. In the "From the Expert" section for this chapter, Kerry Weinger, a partner in Baker & McKenzie LLP, highlights some of the legal questions that can arise when preparing contracts. Kerry believes not only that a formal contract is necessary but also that consultants should engage the services of an attorney when drawing up a contract or a letter of agreement. There are benefits to working with an attorney who specializes in consulting contracts; such an attorney can help with the wording of the contract as well as assist with the handling of issues such as confidentiality and copyrights. Kerry emphasizes the importance of communicating clearly with your client both in writing and verbally, especially with regard to the scope of the work to be performed, the fees or rate schedules, expenses, service-level agreements, and completion dates.

Although a contract between you and a client does not have to be highly formal and prepared by an attorney (although that may be very desirable in many situations), you and a client have a contract when both of you agree, even orally, that you will provide a service in exchange for a payment. As you will see, many consultants send clients letters of agreement that serve as both a proposal and, when both parties sign, a contract. We discuss contracts and legal issues at greater length later in this chapter.

From the Experts ...
The Importance of Written Contracts
by Kerry Weinger, Partner, Baker & McKenzie LLP

Having a strong, flexible contract is the foundation for a strong consultant–client relationship. There are several legal concerns that can arise during the course of the relationship, and these need to be addressed in the contract.

Each agreement needs to be customized depending on the person and company with whom you will be working, although you may want to begin with a template, or standard agreement.

Often, the prospective client will have a standard agreement that either the prospective client or the prospective client's attorney has prepared. Be wary of such agreements and review them carefully. Frequently, they are vague or contain provisions slanted in the prospective client's favor. Likewise, standard agreements may not contain provisions essential for your protection.

If the prospective client insists on using its standard agreement, discuss any concerns you have with the prospective client. Remember, terms are negotiable. If the prospective client has issued a purchase order, be sure to confirm that it does not supersede or conflict with any part of the written agreement you and the client have.

Standard agreements often contain provisions that you may find objectionable. For example, it may say that the consultant will not work for any of the prospective client's competitors during the project and for a period of 1 year or more after the project is completed. If you're inclined to accept such a provision, you may want assurances that you will receive work from the prospective client in the future or other income to compensate for agreeing to this noncompetition clause. To assuage a prospective client who is persistent about including this provision, consider negotiating to replace the clause with a confidentiality provision. This provides the client with protection from disclosure of its proprietary information.

The prospective client's standard agreement may also contain a section that any disagreement should be resolved close to the prospective client's physical location, such as at the home office. To reduce your exposure to the costs of retaining legal counsel and dealing with the dispute potentially in a far-off location, negotiate that resolution needs to take place closer to your physical place of business. Alternatively, it may be more cost-efficient, and resolution of the dispute quicker to achieve, if you insert a clause stating that arbitration, rather than litigation, will be used to resolve disputes.

Letters of Agreement

Having defined proposals and contracts, that leaves the third term, *letter of agreement*. Consultants often prepare letters of agreement instead of formal contracts, particularly for small projects.

In the typical consulting arrangement, the consultant discusses a project with the client, and they arrive at an understanding as to how the project will be handled as well as what the consultant will be paid. The consultant then prepares a short (one- or two-page) letter, usually on the consultant's letterhead, outlining the agreed-on terms. The consultant then signs the letter and sends it to the client. If the client agrees to the contents, he or she signs the letter also. The presence of both signatures makes the document legally binding (technically, a contract), and the work can begin.

The reason letters of agreement are used so often is that they are very convenient. For example, if a company has a small project it wants to undertake, it doesn't make sense for the company (or the consultant) to spend a lot of time developing an RFP, reviewing proposals, and then hiring lawyers to prepare and review contracts. The cost for that lengthy process could be one hundred times the cost of the project itself. Instead, many consultants and their clients simply prepare letters of agreement that cover the important points of both a proposal and a contract in a short, easily constructed document.

CHOOSING A FORMAT

Which format you will use—a formal contract or a letter of agreement—depends primarily on the client's requirements and expectations. Government agencies, for example, usually require consultants to submit formal proposals that conform to agency-specific guidelines. By contrast, most private sector organizations accept brief letters of agreement in lieu of a formal contract. However, for a large, complex project, even a small company may require a lengthy, detailed proposal to ensure that both parties are in agreement on the project's many details. Frequently, formal contracts are also required if the consultant will be privy to proprietary information or products, whether already in use or being developed. Clients are obviously concerned about protecting such information and products and will use the contract to ensure that they are covered for all manner of contingencies.

Companies, government agencies, and individual clients have different preferences and different rules. Before sitting down to write a proposal, find out what the client expects. Consultants often describe the format they usually use for proposals and ask whether that format is satisfactory for the project being discussed. Alternatively, you may want to ask the client what information is needed, in how much detail, and in what format. You may also ask for a sample proposal that exemplifies the preferred format and length. Your request may not be granted, but it is sometimes worth asking if you are confused about the format of the proposal or contract the client expects.

LEGAL CONSIDERATIONS

As we have noted, all proposals and letters of agreement become legally binding once both parties agree to and sign the document. In the following section we address some, although by no means all, of the questions about contracts that arise in the practice of consulting.

When is a contract legally valid? For a contract to be legally valid, two conditions must be met. First, there must be *mutual consent*, and second, there must be *valid consideration*.

Mutual Consent

Both sides must enter into a contract freely and by their own choosing. Contracts cannot be one sided, with one party deciding what the other will do without the (freely given) agreement of the second party. A document is not legally binding if one of the parties was coerced, or misled, or simply never agreed to the terms of the document.

Valid Consideration

Each party to the contract must receive something of value. A contract is not binding unless each party receives something that would be deemed to have value in a court of law. In the consulting business, the consultant usually provides a service to the client, and the client, in exchange, provides financial remuneration to the consultant.

ORAL OR WRITTEN CONTRACTS

Are oral agreements valid contracts? An oral contract can be as legally binding as a written one. Indeed, many of the contracts we agree to every day fall into this category. A person who cuts someone's grass or cleans her apartment probably has an oral contract to perform that service. In exchange, the person performing the service expects a specific, agreed-on payment.

Many consulting contracts are based on oral agreements, particularly if the client and the consultant are both in-house employees. For example, the vice president of sales might well ask an internal consultant to help plan and facilitate a retreat for the members of the sales department. The consultant would probably agree to assist (it is not wise to say no to a vice president). The consultant's remuneration would more than likely be the consultant's regular salary, so the matter of fees would be a nonissue. Given this situation, it is more than likely that neither party would even consider formalizing the arrangement.

Recently, however, many companies are using written contracts even when both parties work for the same company. Some of this stems from a growing emphasis on the exchange of payments and accountability for intradepartmental services. Thus, if a manufacturing unit wants the line employees trained on Six Sigma, it may have to pay the company's internal training unit, much as it would pay an external firm, to provide the training.

Another reason for the increased frequency of written contracts even between coworkers is that oral contracts are a recipe for potential problems. Sometimes people do not remember the details of what they agreed on, especially if the two parties discussed the project in January and work is not in full swing until June. Or, as occasionally happens, the manager who made the oral agreement with the consultant may have left the company and never told the replacement what the agreement entailed.

For these reasons, all agreements should be put in writing, regardless of whether you are working as an internal or an external consultant. A short memo often suffices; sometimes, a somewhat more formal letter of agreement or proposal is necessary; finally, complex projects may well require a lengthy contract, drawn up by an attorney from the client's legal department. Regardless of the format of the document, both parties should acknowledge verbally and in writing that they accept the terms and should retain copies of the agreement.

There are other compelling reasons to always prepare detailed legal contracts. For example, does the work involve copyright or patent issues? Will products be developed during the project? Are there questions about who will have the rights to the products? Are there questions of liability? In short, if there any legal issues related to your work (and there often are), seek the counsel of an attorney and having the attorney prepare a contract. (As noted earlier, the client often has a company attorney do this.)

In addition to the legal advantages of having a written agreement, the process of preparing the document forces both parties to clarify exactly what results they expect from the project and from each other. If there are questions down the line about the terms on which the two parties agreed, or about any other details, the written agreement should provide the answer. If changes are necessary once the project is underway, a memo describing the changes, signed by both parties, should satisfy a legal challenge.

Contract Disputes

Consultants frequently are concerned about their legal recourse in the event that the client does not honor the oral or written contract. As in most conflicts between two parties in a service relationship, you should first try to work out the disagreement with the client directly. If this approach is not successful, then going the legal route and hiring an attorney to pursue your interests is certainly an option. Rarely do consultants pursue the legal route, however. Most think that taking legal action simply takes too much time, effort, and money.

Now that we have defined the important terms and provided insight on some of the legal concerns, let's begin learning how to write a good proposal.

CONTENTS OF A GOOD PROPOSAL

The rest of this chapter focuses on the writing of proposals (which are similar to letters of agreement), as this is the critical part of formalizing your agreement with a prospective client. A well-defined and clear proposal, one that describes the major parts of the consulting project, is the key to successful consulting. Moreover, having a well-constructed proposal will eliminate at least 90% of the problems that are likely to arise during a consulting assignment. So, let's begin.

What should be in the proposal? As noted earlier, the answer depends on the nature of the project and the client's requirements. However, here are the basics. At the very least, a proposal must contain a few sentences about the problem being investigated or the project being undertaken. It must also include a little information about the consultant's approach to handling the problem or project, as well as the major activities the consultant will perform, how long the project will take, and the client's fee to do the work.

Beyond the basic information, proposals vary considerably. Some contain statements concerning confidentiality, patent rights, who can terminate the contract, noncompetition clauses, and other issues of concern to the client and the consultant. The following list provides an overview of the issues most often covered in proposals:

- Why is the proposal being submitted? Define the challenges being faced and the expected benefits of the proposed project. An explanation of how results will be measured is sometimes included.
- What work will be performed? This is the core of the proposal. What activities or tasks will both you and the client perform to accomplish the desired outcomes?
- What are your responsibilities? Given the work that has been outlined, what tasks will you complete?
- What are the client's responsibilities? What support is the client expected to offer? Will personnel be provided? What action is the client expected to initiate in association with the project?
- What is the timeline for the project? When will it start? How long will it take?

- What fees and costs will the client incur? What is the schedule of payment?
- What are your qualifications to perform the work? This question usually is addressed in a brief statement to indicate that the consultant has the experience and skills to make the project a success.

The following issues are less frequently included in proposals but should be if the project is complex and lengthy:

- *Confidentiality and/or anonymity statements.* Including an anonymity statement is a way to assure the client that the sources of information will not be disclosed. A confidentiality statement assures the client that the consultant will not disclose information about the company gathered as part of the consulting project.
- *Statements about reporting procedures.* Some proposals include a paragraph about the nature and number of reports the consultant is expected to produce and who will receive them. Similarly, is the consultant expected to provide progress briefings and, if so, how often and to whom?
- *Contract termination.* Why and how may one or both parties terminate the contract?
- *Rights to materials.* Who has the legal right to materials and instruments developed as part of the project?
- *Detailed information about the consulting firm and/or the biographies of the key consultants who will be working on the project.* This may be included in an appendix. This information is usually included to convince the client that the firm or group of consultants has the depth of experience to execute the project successfully.
- *Other support materials.* Some proposals require extensive support materials, such as the survey questionnaire to be used, training materials to be used, research findings, drawings, and planning diagrams. These materials usually are put in an appendix.

FEES

One of the questions consultants most frequently ask is how much they should charge for their services and on what basis these charges should be set. We touch on a couple of points on fees here.

Most consultants charge an hourly or a daily rate. Daily fees vary considerably, making it difficult to suggest what an appropriate fee might be. Consultants who work with religious groups and churches may charge as little as $150 to $300 per day, whereas the rate in the private sector is typically between $800 and $3,200 per day. More established consultants charge daily rates of $1,500 to $5,000, and a few premier consultants charge considerably more.

Direct expenses, such as travel, hotel accommodations, and materials (none of which are taxable) are often billed separately. These expenses are usually itemized, and the consultant may be required to submit the original receipts. Whether these direct expenses are reimbursed or are part of the daily rate should be clarified in the proposal.

As an alternative to hourly or daily rates, some consultants prefer to charge fixed, or project fees. Many large consulting firms use this method. With the fixed-fee method, the consultant contracts to complete the entire project for an agreed-on amount. If the project is completed at or under what the consultant has budgeted for the project, the consultant could make a nice profit. However, if the time needed to complete the project, or the costs, have been miscalculated, the consultant can end up losing money. In general, consultants who use a fixed-fee approach earn higher incomes than those who charge by the day or hour.

To calculate a fixed fee one must first estimate how much time it will take to complete the project. This figure is then multiplied by the hourly or daily fee the consultant would like to receive. Finally, costs such as office overhead and insurance are added in. As noted earlier, some consultants include direct expenses, such as travel and lodging, in their fixed fees. Others prefer to bill for these expenses separately, because some direct costs, such as airfare, are difficult to predict over long time periods. Regardless of how the calculations are done, the consultant has to be adept at estimating time and costs to come out ahead.

Considerable thought should be given to establishing the time involved in a project. Establishing a timeline, working backward, and delineating each day's activities is a helpful way to determine the expected hours needed to complete a project.

Once the costs have been estimated, plus an estimate of the time the project will take multiplied by the consultant's daily rate, the next step is to decide the amount of profit to add on to the project. When that amount has been determined, add this amount to the total, and the result is the (fixed) fee that you will charge the client to complete the work.

Several other approaches to billing are used, although less frequently than the methods just discussed. For example, if the consultant and client have a *cost-plus-fixed fee* contract, they both estimate (and agree to) the costs of the project and agree to add a fixed fee for the consultant's services. If the consultant is very good at controlling costs, such an arrangement can be profitable.

Performance contracts are yet another option. With this arrangement, the consultant receives a percentage of whatever savings were realized by virtue of his or her work. Thus, if you saved the client $1 million in the first year of the project, you might receive 30% of the first-year savings, which would be $300,000. Although this may look like a very attractive payment system, the consultant makes nothing, not even the cost for expenses, if he or she has not saved the client any money.

WRITING THE PROPOSAL

Assuming you have asked, and received answers to, the questions we outlined in chapter 2; taken good notes; and paid close attention in discussions with the client, writing the proposal should be quite simple. Following a few fairly easy steps should ensure that it comes together quickly.

Let's assume that you have decided that the proposal should be in the form of a short letter of agreement consisting of nine sections. The next step is to write the title of each section on blank sheets of paper. Thus, for our example, we would use nine sheets. Next, for each section, jot down any applicable information. These are just rough notes and can include statistical data, cost estimates, specifications, time lines, and quotations. Most of this information will probably have been generated from your initial interviews with the client and will form the backbone of the proposal.

Just before putting together the proposal, many consultants schedule a meeting with the client, either in person or by telephone, to make sure they are clear on what the client wants. They explain to the client that they are about to write the proposal and are just checking to make sure they have included all the important points. They then go through each section of the proposal, explaining to the client what they are thinking of putting into that section, and check to be sure the information is correct. Figure 3.1 is an outline of how to prepare for and participate in such a meeting.

Meetings to review the contents of the proposal may be brief or lengthy, depending on how much the client wants to add. The advantage of having such a meeting is that you and the client reach agreement on what the proposal should include (and what needs to be accomplished during the project) before the proposal is written up. Prospective clients should feel that they have written the document with you, and, not surprisingly, consultants who use this technique claim it increases their chances of being awarded contracts.

To illustrate how best to proceed with the writing, we use as an example a project for which the consulting group Logistics Inc. is preparing a proposal. Logistics specializes in designing distribution systems for the retail industry. Its clients could be K-Mart, Best Buy, Home Depot, or similar large retail companies. For now, let's assume that Logistics is preparing a letter of agreement for a fictitious corporation called Concart, which recently decentralized its distribution system. Concart is planning to move its distribution centers closer to its retail outlets, which will enable stock to

---

Before the meeting

- Review your notes on the company, particularly what the client has said about the project and how it is to be implemented.
- Outline the major points to be included in each section of the proposal.
- Develop an agenda.

During the meeting

- Identify and clarify the nature of the project or problem.
- Identify and confirm what the prospective client thinks a successful project will entail and what it will accomplish.
- Identify the expected deliverables or outcomes and timeline expectations.
- Discuss and confirm the approach or methodology.
- Clarify your responsibilities and resource requirements.
- Clarify the client's responsibilities and resource requirements.
- Discuss reporting requirements and the timeline for project updates.
- Discuss costs and fees, including all resource requirements such as office space, equipment, and/or people.
- For each of the preceding, confirm with the client that what you are including in the proposal meets with the client's approval.
- Ask if there is anything else the client would like you to put in the proposal.

After the meeting

- Submit the proposal.

FIG. 3.1.   Checklist for proposal/contract meetings.

---

be replenished in the outlets within 1 day. Concart's marketing objective is to assure its customers that they will always find the products they need in stock at a Concart store. Unfortunately, the strategy looks better on paper than it does in the distribution centers, so Concart has asked Logistics Inc. to discover why decentralizing the distribution system has not led to higher sales volume.

As in our previous example, the proposal Logistics Inc. prepares for Concart consists of nine sections:

1. Address, salutation, and introductory paragraph
2. Objectives and expected benefits
3. Background
4. Project plan

5. Timetable
6. Confidentiality
7. Project costs and terms
8. Qualifications
9. Ending and signatures

We have already prepared some notes for each of these sections, so it is time to start writing. We discuss each section separately and then show you the complete proposal in Fig. 3.2, Sample Proposal.

Section 1: Introductory Paragraph

A proposal between a consulting firm and a company usually begins with the date, the client's name and address, and the salutation. Let's imagine that the consultants at Logistics Inc. have had several lengthy discussions about the project with several people at Concart. It is important in writing the proposal to restate any verbal agreements Logistics Inc. and Concart have already reached. Having achieved a consensus *before* writing the proposal is ideal.

The introductory paragraph usually indicates something to the effect that the consultant appreciates the opportunity to submit the proposal and is confident the methods described will resolve whatever problem the client is having. Thus, the introductory paragraph in Logistics' proposal for Concart might read like this:

This proposal is a summary of the points we agreed upon in our April 21 confer-
ence call to discuss the forthcoming project regarding Concart's process of re-
plenishing its inventory. Logistics Inc. thanks you for the opportunity to discuss
the challenges facing the distribution system at Concart. We recognize the highly
competitive nature of your industry and the critical role of the distribution cen-
ters to your future. We feel confident that the methods outlined in this proposal
will uncover the root of the problems facing the centers and that together we will
be able to redesign the system to meet your performance needs.

Section 2: Objectives and Expected Benefits

The next section states the objectives of the project as well as the expected benefits of conducting the project. This section usually is fairly brief, al- though if the consultant thinks that there will be multiple benefits, they should all be listed. Occasionally this section is labeled *Objectives and Mea- surement*, in which case it includes a statement of the objective(s) as well as how progress, or the success of the project, is to be measured.

In the Logistics case, the objective is clear: Concart wants to be able to ensure next-day delivery of its inventory. The consultants decide to label this section *Project Objectives*, to include a couple of sentences indicating that they understand the source of the inventory problem, and to end with a statement such as the following:

To compete effectively in today's business environment, Concart decentralized its distribution centers a year ago. However, the decentralization has been only partially successful, and several unresolved issues remain that are preventing Concart's distribution centers from operating at their full effectiveness. Logistics Inc. understands that Concart's main objective is to document the logistics problems currently being experienced in your distribution centers across the country and to redesign the inventory-replenishment process in order to achieve next-day delivery of inventory to the retail outlets with 99+% efficiency.

Note that Logistics has not guaranteed that Concart will achieve 99% next-day delivery; instead, it has stated that this is the client's objective.

Section 3: Background

This section contains a brief summary of the conditions that led to the initiation of the project or the reasons the project is necessary. The aim here is to demonstrate an understanding of the problems or concerns that led the client to hire a consultant. The following is an example, demonstrating Logistics' knowledge of relevant background information related to Concart's history:

Concart has been a very successful retailing company that has been adding approximately 80 retail outlets per year nationally. To keep pace with this growth, and to become more competitive, Concart began a program last year to decentralize its distribution system. The objective is to move the centers closer to the retail outlets so as to provide next-day inventory replenishment. Implementation has been only partially successful. The new system seems to work better in the smaller centers than in the larger ones; however, all the facilities seem to be experiencing common problems. The electronic information system that moves information from outlet to supplier and distribution center appears to be working effectively. The major source of the problem seems to be one of logistics at the distribution centers—specifically involving the reception, selecting, repackaging, and delivery of goods to the outlets. It is this problem that Logistics Inc undertakes to resolve.

Section 4: Project Plan

The next section, sometimes labeled *Methodology* or *Work Plan*, is one of the most important in the proposal. It is the foundation of the contract between the client and the consultant: the outline of what the consultant will do and what the client will receive in return for paying the consultant. A hypothetical example of Logistics' proposal might read like this:

There are four critical players in the replenishment system at Concart: retail outlets; product suppliers; distribution centers; and the logistics center in Atlanta, which is responsible for designing and maintaining the distribution system. All four of these players will have to be involved in identifying and correcting the current problems in the system; however, the focus of our study will be on activities taking place in the distribution centers.

We propose that the project be conducted in several steps. First, our consultants will spend approximately 3 days at the logistics center in Atlanta. The purpose of this visit will be to familiarize them with the way the system is currently designed, as well as the performance objectives for the system. Next, we will conduct site visits to a cross-section of the distribution centers; if a center is not visited, a telephone interview will be conducted with the manager of the center. In addition, we will conduct several telephone interviews with suppliers and with retail outlets. The purpose of these interviews/visits will be to understand the nature of the problems occurring in the system and to elicit suggestions on how the problems might be corrected.

As part of the above step, we will develop several case study examples of centers that have encountered problems with the replenishment process. These cases will map the flow of information and of product, beginning with the stock-replenishment order and ending with delivery of the product to the retail outlet. This mapping process will identify where, and why, the process is breaking down.

Using data collected from the above studies, we will prepare a report analyzing and summarizing the problems and identifying the causes. This report will be presented at a 2-day design workshop conducted with a cross-section of the managers of Concart's distribution centers, several key suppliers, and personnel from Concart's logistics center. The purpose of this workshop will be to review the preparations for redesigning the logistics system so that the problems will be corrected and the system will be able to ensure a 99% rate of next-day replenishment of inventory. Our consultants will facilitate this meeting and will offer our recommendations for system improvement. Our consultants will also assume responsibility for writing the plan that emerges from this session.

The proposed plan for correcting the replenishment system will be reviewed with key suppliers and a group of managers of the retail outlets. We will coordinate this effort. Any corrections will be incorporated into the plan. The revised plan, together with an estimate of the costs associated with it, will then be presented to Concart's executive committee for approval. We will assist you in developing this presentation. The decision about who will make the presentation will be decided after further discussion.

This will end the phase of the project described in this proposal. Given approval by the executive committee, the next phase will involve implementation. We are ready to assist you in the implementation phase, and, as discussed, we will submit a proposal for the implementation phase as soon as the scope and details of this phase become clear.

Section 5: Timetable

After the work to be performed has been described, the next section outlines the timeframe for getting that work accomplished. This section is usually labeled *Timetable, Time Schedule,* or *Work Schedule*. Included in this section should be information such as when the consultant will begin work on the project and when major activities will be completed. If the client has not provided enough information to project these dates, the consultant may simply indicate the amount of time needed to complete the project and when the consultant is able to start. In the following sample section, we note how Logistics might deal with this issue in its proposal to Concart:

We are very aware of the urgency of this project and are able to begin work on it at the Atlanta logistics center on April 23. During that week, we will also arrange for the phone interviews and visits with suppliers, distribution centers, and retail outlets and should be able to begin that phase on April 30.

The interviews and analysis will take approximately 3 weeks, and the 2-day design session described above will be scheduled for the last week in May. We are confident that a viable plan will emerge from that meeting that could be presented to the executive committee at their June 15 meeting. Given the committee's approval, implementation could start immediately.

Section 6: Confidentiality

Confidentiality agreements are not always necessary in proposals or letters of agreement. One must be included in Logistics' proposal to Concart because its new inventory-replenishment system will presumably provide Concart with a competitive advantage over other retailers. Providing the client with assurance that Logistics' consultants will not disclose any information about Concart, Concart's suppliers, or the system is extremely important. Including a short statement such as the following usually provides the assurance the client needs:

Given the sensitivity of the information we will be working with, we assure Concart that we will not directly or indirectly disclose or use, either during or after the project, any information about the project or about Concart or its suppliers without prior written consent.

Section 7: Project Costs and Terms

This section, sometimes labeled *Terms and Conditions, Project Budget, Fees and Payments,* or *Project Costs and Terms,* details the costs the client will incur in undertaking the project as well as the conditions of payment. As indicated earlier in this chapter, fees may be calculated in several ways. The two most frequently used methods are to charge by the day or to charge a set amount for the entire project. In either case, costs for travel, hotel accommodations, meals, and other such expenses are billed separately. It is customary to ask for payment of 33% to 50% of the total fee at the time the contract is signed and the rest in periodic installments or at the end of the project.

Let's assume for the moment that Logistics has estimated that it will take three consultants 19 days, or a total of 57 days, to complete the project for Concart. Assuming that Logistics has a standard rate that it charges for work like it will be doing for Concart, Logistics would simply indicate its day rate, the number of consultants who will be working on the project, and the number of days Logistics anticipates it will need to complete the project. In calculating this rate, Logistics will have taken into account a number of costs, such as rent and other overhead expenses to operate its office, advertising, and so forth. Although these expenses should be considered in arriving at a day rate, they should not be itemized in the proposal. In fact, most independent consultants do not even bother to figure out their overhead but bill at the going rate. In larger firms, overhead expenses are simply reflected in their higher daily fees.

Having evaluated the pros and cons of using a day rate versus charging a project fee, Logistics has decided to bill on a project basis. This is determined by multiplying the total number of consultant days devoted to the project (57) by the amount the firm pays its consultants per day in salary. In calculating this figure, many firms add in overhead expenses as well as a 15% profit margin. Many also add a little cushion (several hundred to several thousand dollars, depending on the size of the project and the potential for miscellaneous expenses) to cover contingencies. For the sake of our example, let's assume that the resulting project fee came to $140,000. Logistics included a statement to this effect in its proposal:

Our professional fee to conduct the project as outlined above is $140,000. In addition, you will be billed for all direct expenses associated with the project. These include costs associated with travel (airfare, hotels, meals, and ground transportation), as well as for long-distance telephone calls, overnight express, photocopying, and other costs associated with the execution of the project. Normally such reimbursable charges are about 20% to 25% of the total professional fee.

Upon your authorization to begin the project, 50% of the professional fees cited above will be billed. The remaining 50% ($70,000) will be invoiced monthly. Reimbursable expenses incurred during the course of the project will be invoiced monthly as well.

Section 8: Qualifications

The section labeled *Qualifications* or *Credentials* is where you explain why you or the firm for which you work is the best qualified to do the job. If you have successfully completed projects similar to the one the client wants to do, this is the place to mention that, particularly if those projects were in the client's industry. For example, if the project involves installing a quality-assurance system for a hospital, you would certainly want to mention if you have had great success installing similar systems in other hospitals. You might want to identify the hospitals, too (assuming you have permission from the hospital to do so). Most important, you need to demonstrate competency to handle the proposed work.

Logistics specializes in designing distribution systems and has considerable experience in this area. Wisely, Logistics includes examples in its proposal for Concart:

> *Logistics Inc. has more than 20 years of experience designing, upgrading, and maintaining distribution systems. Our primary field of consulting is logistics, and all our consultants are experts in this field. We have completed more than 300 projects, making us one of the premier logistics consulting firms in the country. We have worked for the top retail organizations in the United States, Canada, and Europe and have completed several other successful projects for Concart.*

If a firm uses a unique problem-solving technique, the section on credentials is the place to discuss it. Or, for example, if several of the firm's consultants have worked in positions directly related to the project—such as, in this case, as distribution managers in the retail industry—or have designed the distribution system for a large company, such as Wal-Mart, this is the section in which to mention it. What is most important is to outline the skills and background that make you or the consultants in your firm uniquely qualified to succeed with this project.

Some consulting firms include an appendix containing biographies of the consultants who will be working on a project. Although some consultants question whether this practice is effective, excellent credentials are likely to impress, and the appendix is the best place for such information. Including them cannot hurt (unless the consultants are seriously underqualified for the job), and including them sometimes gives a firm an edge over a competitor. Given two proposals that are similar in content, clients often make the final decision based on a review of the consultants' credentials.

Section 9: Ending

In the final section of the proposal you usually express your eagerness to work with the company and your confidence that the client's objectives will be met if you or the firm you represent is hired. As shown in the following excerpt, there is usually a statement to the effect that the prospective client should sign the proposal if the conditions are agreeable and return a copy to you or your firm:

We look forward to working with Concart and are confident that by working together we can make a positive difference in your distribution system.

If the terms and conditions of this proposal are acceptable to you, please return a signed copy and retain a copy for your files. Again, we look forward to working with you on this project.

The client may accept the proposal as is or request revisions. If the client accepts the proposal, or accepts the proposal with revisions, the client should indicate this in writing, either on the proposal or on a contract or formal letter of agreement.

Some consultants request formal letters of acceptance. Alternatively, the client or the consultant may draw up a formal contract, written in legal language, that covers the same points as are covered in the proposal. Both parties sign this document. Some consultants enclose an invoice for their first payment along with the signed contract.

Proposal to Increase the Effectiveness of Concart's Distribution Centers by Logistics Inc.

This proposal is summarizes the points we agreed upon in our April 21 conference call to discuss the forthcoming project regarding Concart's procedure for replenishing its inventory. Logistics Inc. thanks you for the opportunity to discuss the challenges facing the distribution system at Concart. We recognize the highly competitive nature of your industry, and the critical role of the distribution centers to your future. We feel confident that the methods outlined in this proposal will uncover the root of the problems facing the centers and that together we will be able to redesign the system to meet your performance needs.

Objectives and Expected Benefits

To compete effectively in today's business environment, Concart decentralized its distribution centers a year ago. However, the decentralization has been only partially successful and several unresolved issues remain that are preventing Concart's distribution centers from operating at their full effectiveness. Logistics, Inc. understands that Concart's main objective is to document the logistics problems currently being experienced in your distribution centers across the country, and to redesign the inventory-replenishment process in order to achieve next-day delivery of inventory to the retail outlets with 99+% efficiency.

Background

Concart has been a very successful retailing company that has been adding approximately 80 retail outlets per year nationally. To keep pace with this growth, and to become more competitive, Concart began a program last year to decentralize its distribution system. The objective is to move the centers closer to the retail outlets so as to provide next-day inventory replenishment. Implementation has been only a partial success. The new system seems to work better in the smaller centers than in the larger ones; however, all the facilities seem to be experiencing common problems. The electronic information system that moves information from outlet to supplier and distribution center appears to be working effectively. The major source of the problem seems to be one of logistics at the distribution centers—specifically involving the reception, selecting, repackaging, and delivery of goods to the outlets. It is this problem that Logistics, Inc. undertakes to resolve.

Project Plan

There are four critical players in the replenishment system at Concart: retail outlets; product suppliers; distribution centers; and the logistics center in Atlanta, which is responsible for designing and maintaining the distribution system. All four of these players will have to be involved in identifying and correcting the current problems in the system; however, the focus of our study will be on activities taking place in the distribution centers.

We propose that the project be conducted in several steps. First, our consultants will spend approximately 3 days at the logistics center in Atlanta. The purpose of this visit will be to familiarize them with the way the system is currently designed, as well as the performance objectives for the system. Next, we will conduct site visits to a cross-section of the distribution centers; if a center is not visited, a telephone interview will be conducted with the manager of the center. In addition, we will conduct several telephone interviews with suppliers and with retail outlets. The purpose of these interviews/visits will be to understand the nature of the problems occurring in the system and to elicit suggestions on how the problems might be corrected.

As part of the above step, we will develop several case study examples of centers that have encountered problems with the replenishment process. These cases will map the flow of information and of product, beginning with the stock-replenishment order and ending with delivery of the product to the retail outlet. This mapping process will identify where, and why, the process is breaking down.

Using data collected from the above studies, we will prepare a report analyzing and summarizing the problems and identifying the causes. This report will be presented at a 2-day design workshop conducted with a cross-section of the managers of Concart's distribution centers, several key

(continued)

suppliers, and personnel from Concart's logistics center. The purpose of this workshop will be to review the preparations for redesigning the logistics system so that the problems will be corrected and the system will be able to ensure a 99% rate of next-day replenishment of inventory. Our consultants will facilitate this meeting and will offer our recommendations for system improvement. Our consultants will also assume responsibility for writing the plan that emerges from this session.

The proposed plan for correcting the replenishment system will be reviewed with key suppliers and a group of managers of the retail outlets. We will coordinate this effort. Any corrections will be incorporated into the plan. The revised plan, together with an estimate of the costs associated with it, will then be presented to Concart's executive committee for approval. We will assist you in developing this presentation. The decision about who will make the presentation will be decided after further discussion.

This will end the phase of the project described in this proposal. Given approval by the executive committee, the next phase will involve implementation. We are ready to assist you in the implementation phase, and, as discussed, we will submit a proposal for the implementation phase as soon as the scope and details of this phase become clear.

Timetable

We are very aware of the urgency of this project and are able to begin work on it at the Atlanta logistics support center on April 23. During that week, we will also arrange for the phone interviews and visits with suppliers, distribution centers, and retail outlets and should be able to begin that phase on April 30.

The interviews and analysis will take approximately 3 weeks, and the 2-day design session described above will be scheduled for the last week in May. We are confident that a viable plan will emerge from that meeting which could be presented to the executive committee at its June 15 meeting. Given the committee's approval, implementation could start immediately.

Confidentiality

Given the sensitivity of the information we will be working with, we assure Concart that we will not directly or indirectly disclose or use, either during or after the project, any information about the project or about Concart or its suppliers without prior written consent.

Project Costs and Terms

Our professional fee to conduct the project as outlined above is $140,000. In addition, you will be billed for all direct expenses associated with the project. These include costs associated with travel (airfare, hotels, meals, and ground transportation), as well as for long-distance telephone calls, overnight express, photocopying, and other costs associated with the execution of the project. Normally such reimbursable charges are about 20% to 25% of the total professional fee.

Upon your authorization to begin the project, 50% of the professional fees cited above will be billed. The remaining 50% ($70,000) will be invoiced monthly. Reimbursable expenses incurred during the course of the project will be invoiced monthly as well.

Qualifications

Logistics, Inc. has more than 20 years of experience designing, upgrading, and maintaining distribution systems. Our primary field of consulting is logistics, and all our consultants are experts in this field. We have completed more than 300 projects, making us one of the premier logistics consulting firms in the country. We have worked for the top retail organizations in the United States, Canada, and Europe and have completed several other successful projects for Concart.

Summary

We look forward to working with Concart and are confident that by working together we can make a positive difference in your distribution system.

If the terms and conditions of this proposal are acceptable to you, please return a signed copy and retain a copy for your files. Again, we look forward to working with you on this project.

Sincerely,
Gary Brown
Partner, Logistics, Inc.
Please sign and date:

Ms. Mary Moran,
Director, Concart International, Inc.
Signature and date _____

Gary Brown,
Partner, Logistics, Inc.
Signature and date _____

FIG. 3.2.   Full sample proposal.

INTERNAL AGREEMENTS

Internal proposals or contracts for work done by internal consultants for their employers are usually much less formal than those external consultants prepare. Since the work is being handled internally, there is usually less concern about liability, patent rights, confidentiality, fees, or payment schedules. Most internal proposals are in the form of informal memos that include a brief description of what the consultant(s) will do for the client, the schedule for doing it, and what type of support the client will provide.

This is not to suggest that the memo shouldn't cover the basics. The objectives should certainly be clearly stated, project activities and a schedule for the completion of activities should be described in some detail, and the accountabilities of both the client and consultant should be outlined. Even with internal projects, it is important to put the details in writing so that both parties will have a record of the activities to be conducted and when and who has responsibility for what. See Fig. 3.3 for a sample internal agreement.

As with more formal proposals, we recommend that both parties sign and date the agreement. This will ensure (or at least, better ensure) that both parties understand what the project will entail, how the work will be accomplished, and what each party's responsibilities and obligations are, as well the time line for the project. Often managers just skim internal memos, assuming that they know the content. Having both parties sign the agreement helps ensure that both parties read the memo carefully. And this helps to eliminate misunderstandings once the project is under way.

FOLLOW-UP MEETINGS

After a proposal has been submitted, some consultants arrange to meet with clients in person or by phone to go over the proposal and to ensure that the client understands and agrees with the details and conditions. These meetings are usually brief and informal and are presented to the client as an opportunity to make sure everything is in order and to their specifications. You might want to note that ironing out details is more efficient face to face (or over the phone) than exchanging notes or e-mails. Also, if the client wants changes, they can be made immediately.

Some consultants routinely hold meetings after they submit a proposal, but others think they are unnecessary and a waste of time. Their argument is that if a consultant has done a good job of involving the client in the development of project strategy and has been sensitive to the client's wants and needs up to this point, then the client has already agreed to the terms of the proposal and further discussion is unnecessary. We suspect that it comes down to how confident the consultant feels about the details of the proposal. If you feel confident that all the details have been worked out, then you are likely to think that an additional meeting is unnecessary. However, if points remain on which you and the client have not reached agreement, a meeting after you have sent the prospective client the proposal offers a chance to resolve any lingering issues. Alternatively, if several consultants are bidding on a project, then a meeting with the prospective client can be a useful opportunity to sell the proposal.

To: Mary Moran, Director of Operations, Logistics Center, Concart
          International, Inc.
From: Brayden Gregory, Internal Consulting Department, Concart
          International, Inc.
Date: 7/8/06
Re: Proposal To Increase Effectiveness of Concart's Distribution
          Centers

This memo summarizes the points we agreed upon in our April 21 meeting, in which we discussed the forthcoming project regarding Concart's process of replenishing its inventory. We feel confident that the methods outlined in this memo will uncover the root of the problems facing the centers and that together we will be able to redesign the system to meet our performance needs. We are eager to work with you to redesign the inventory-replenishment process, with the goal of achieving next-day delivery of inventory to the retail outlets with 99+% efficiency.

As we discussed in our April 21 meeting, we propose that the project be conducted in several steps. First, our internal consultants will spend approximately 3 days at the logistics center in Atlanta. The purpose of this visit will be to familiarize our colleagues with the way the system is currently designed, as well as the performance objectives for the system. Next, we will conduct site visits to a cross-section of the distribution centers; if a center is not visited, we will make every effort to conduct a telephone interview with the manager of the center. In addition, we will conduct several telephone interviews with suppliers and with our retail outlets. The purpose of these interviews/visits is to understand the nature of the problems occurring in the system and to elicit suggestions from each stakeholder as to how the problems might be corrected. Using data collected from the above studies, we will prepare a report analyzing and summarizing the problems and identifying the causes.

The proposed plan for correcting the replenishment system will be reviewed with key suppliers and a group of managers of the retail outlets. We will coordinate this effort. Any corrections to our findings will be incorporated into the plan. The revised plan, together with an estimate of the costs associated with our recommendations, will then be presented to Concart's executive committee for approval. We will be glad to assist you in developing this presentation but will assume that you will handle this.

This will end the phase of the project described in this memo. Given approval by the executive committee, the next phase will involve implementation. We will gladly assist you in the implementation phase upon your request. Please let us know if our services are needed in this regard.

We are very aware of the urgency of this project and are able to begin work on it at the Atlanta logistics support center on May 27. During that week, we will also arrange for the phone interviews and visits with suppliers,

(continued)

distribution centers, and retail outlets and should be able to begin that phase on May 30.

We expect the study should be completed in time for presentation at our executive committee's meeting on June 15. If you are in agreement with the project details outlined in this memo, please indicate your agreement and sign and date the memo and return it to me. I, in turn, will sign and send you a copy. I look forward to working with you on this, Mary.

FIG. 3.3.   Sample memo from an internal consultant.

REQUESTING CLIENT FEEDBACK

When an organization receives proposals from several consultants, it is obvious that all but one will probably not receive a contract. That is the reality of the consulting business. However, if your proposal was rejected, the disappointment can be turned into a learning opportunity by receiving feedback from the client. Be sure to ask the contact person within the organization some of the following questions: What did the client think were the strong points of your proposal? What were the weak points? What was it about the accepted proposal that sold the client on awarding the contract to that firm?

Savvy consultants can learn a lot following the loss of a contract, assuming they use the rejection as an opportunity to critically examine their approach and presentation. The trick is to turn the experience into an opportunity to learn how to write better proposals. Some prospective clients will be quite willing to provide feedback; others will not (and may not even return phone calls). Regardless of how willing they are to talk to you, always send your contact at the company a note thanking the person for reviewing your proposal and requesting that people at the company keep you in mind for future projects.

REVISING PROPOSALS

In the best of all worlds, proposals are accepted as is, without requests for any changes. More frequently, a prospective client will ask for revisions. In this case, a meeting to discuss the person's concerns is definitely in order. If you are amenable to the revisions, the proposal is then amended to meet the prospective client's objections and resubmitted (quickly). If you are uncomfortable with the changes and think that agreeing to make them could jeopardize the project, discuss your concerns with the client. Discussing alternative methods to achieve the desired goals is a constructive way of approaching this situation.

If the client insists on changes that you think would jeopardize the project, then you would be wise to end your relationship with the prospective client, at least with regard to this project. Not all proposals have to end in contracts, and sometimes a consultant has to admit that a project cannot be successful given the prospective client's conditions. Being committed in writing to goals one does not believe are possible to achieve is a good predictor of failure. An agreement that is not consummated is much better than an agreement that results in an unsuccessful project. Building and maintaining your reputation should always take precedence over embarking on a questionable client–consultant relationship.

SUMMARY

As should now be evident, the proposal/contract phase of a consulting project needs to be approached thoughtfully and carefully. It is during this phase that you and the client enter into a formal, legally binding agreement that specifies the services you will provide and the client's responsibilities and obligations.

We now offer a few key success factors that should help you ensure that your proposals result in contracts.

KEY SUCCESS FACTORS FOR FORMALIZING THE AGREEMENT

- Fully understand your client's expectations—never lose sight of the fact that it is their goals you are seeking to fulfill, not your own.
- Check with the client as to the preferred format and length for the proposal, as well as any specific issues to be covered.
- Make sure that both your responsibilities and obligations and those of the prospective client are clearly spelled out (and understood) in the proposal and contract.
- Use the proposal format described in this chapter as a checklist to ensure that all the important points are covered.
- Recognize that your proposal is a reflection of you and your company. Devote care and attention to preparing it.
- Maintain the client's confidentiality at all times, as in all phases of the project.
- Try to get feedback on proposals that are not accepted and learn from this feedback.

4

Developing a Project Strategy: Diagnosis and Data Collection

Once your contract is secure, you can finally begin actual work on the project. Don't go too fast, though. Although the proposal and contract outline in general how you should proceed, you still need a thorough action plan or strategy. This entails carefully diagnosing the problem you were brought in to deal with and determining what data need to be collected to ensure that the problem is thoroughly investigated. As discussed in the "From the Expert ..." section in this chapter, data collection begins at the beginning of a project, the moment you talk with a client or prospective client about a potential project.

One useful way to think of the diagnosis and data collection phase of a project is as five interrelated steps: (a) identifying the problem; (b) assessing the data that need to be collected to study the problem; (c) determining where to find these data; (d) deciding how to collect the data; and (e) summarizing, evaluating, and drawing conclusions from the data (see Table 4.1). In this chapter we focus on steps 1 to 4. Step 5 is covered in detail in the next chapter.

Let's begin by examining a somewhat silly example. Suppose your mother just called and said that your favorite but very eccentric aunt has died. She lives 80 miles from Casper, Wyoming, in a gold-mining town. She has no children, and her husband died years ago in a mining accident. The story in the family is that she has amassed a lot of gold, money, and probably both. She always liked you, since you were named after her father, and you figure you might be in line for a big inheritance. You learned of her death on a Wednesday morning while at home in Dallas. In her typical quirky manner, your aunt has stipulated that, to be included in her will, you have to attend her funeral at 9:30 on Friday morning, after which the

TABLE 4.1
Five Steps of Diagnosis and Data Collection

1. Identify the problem. What is the question or problem the client wants solved? What is the "real" problem?
2. What data need to be collected to answer the client's question or to solve the client's problem?
3. Where is this information available? What has to be done to access it? Who has this information?
4. What is the most appropriate way to collect this information?
5. What conclusions can be reached from the information and data that have been collected?

will shall be read. You are not sure you are mentioned in the will, but you are positive you won't be if you don't show up for the funeral.

As with the problems consultants study, you would be wise to ask yourself the following five questions as you evaluate how to get to your aunt's funeral:

1. What is the problem that needs to be solved? You assume it is that you need to get from Dallas to 80 miles from Casper by Friday morning and preferably by Thursday evening to give yourself a little leeway. Otherwise, you risk getting excluded from the will.
2. What information do you need to solve this problem? Plenty, it seems, if you're going to get to your destination quickly. For example, you might check on plane schedules, or train schedules, or the availability of rental cars, or maybe how long it would take you to drive from home.
3. Where is this information available? Who has it? You could call your dentist, who you think visited Casper, but logic would suggest that you would be better to contact the commercial airlines, private charter companies, or car rental companies—in other words, people in the transportation industry.
4. How do you get the information you need? The Internet has a lot of sites that list airline schedules, or you could phone a few airlines or a travel agent. You might even consider phoning the Casper chamber of commerce. This would enable you to learn all the transportation options to this part of the country.
5. What conclusions can you draw based on the options that are available? You should probably pick the means of transportation that is

the most reliable, safest, and certain to get you to the funeral with time to spare. You might also want to choose the least expensive option, just in case your aunt left all her money to her cats.

We warned you that our example was pretty silly, but the point is that the diagnosis and data collection phase of a consulting project has a sequential logic not unlike most models used to solve simple problems. Granted, most consulting problems or assignments are much more complicated than figuring out how to get from Dallas to a funeral near Casper; however, a similar step-by-step logic is applied.

In addition to being more complicated than the problem used in our example, most of the problems consultants face are so varied and different from one another that it is difficult to recommend a technique or approach that applies to all, or even most, of them. That is also what makes consulting so interesting and challenging—and what can make a consultant so valuable to an organization.

To illustrate the diversity of questions faced by consultants, as well as the diversity of methods they use to address these questions, consider the following examples:

• In the last chapter, we discussed a problem facing the managers at Concart, concerning the company's new distribution process, which was not delivering the results management anticipated. What information would a consultant have needed to address this problem? Where was this information located? What data collection method could have been used?

• Later in this chapter we present a case involving a leading U.S. shoe manufacturer that is considering starting an online retail store. What information is needed in this situation? Who has it? What is the best way to collect it?

• Also in this chapter, you will learn about a consumer-products company whose top managers are concerned because many of the company's most promising junior managers are turning down offers to work abroad. What information is needed to evaluate this problem? Who has this information? What is the best way to collect it?

• Finally, and also in this chapter, you will learn about a major hotel chain that introduced several features in an effort to target the business market. The question the client posed for the consultant was whether business travelers liked the special services the hotel chain was offering. What additional services did business travelers want? What information is needed to answer these questions? Who has it? How should this information be collected?

As these examples illustrate, each consulting assignment has unique diagnostic challenges. In the preceding examples, the problems may appear to be fairly obvious and clear cut. In the real world, however, the problem often turns out to be more complicated that it appears. Occasionally, the presenting problem—that is, the problem as the client sees it—is merely a symptom of another problem that is far more difficult to discern. This is one reason it is so important to begin a project by diagnosing the problem thoroughly and carefully. Let's look at each of the five steps of this process.

DEFINING THE PROBLEM

The first step in diagnosing a problem is one of the most important in a consulting project, yet it is also one that is often overlooked. This is because many people involved in a consulting project, including the client, often want to move to data collection and implementation as quickly as possible, on the mistaken assumption that that is when the "real" work gets done. In fact, defining the problem incorrectly can lead to resources being wasted, frequently at great expense, as well as frustration when the proposed solution to the problem has little or no positive effects. Many a consultant has come up with what they thought was a great solution only to discover that they were focusing on the wrong problem or had only partially defined the issue's scope.

Before you can begin data collection or implementation, you need to be able to answer each of the following questions. Only when you can answer each of them have you diagnosed the problem you will be working to solve.

- Is the problem the client has identified the real problem, or is this problem merely a symptom of the problem that really needs to be addressed?
- What information would help define the real problem more clearly?
- What is the real problem the organization is trying to solve, or the question that needs to be answered?
- What is the scope of the issue; that is, what are the questions that need to be addressed in order to solve the problem? What is the primary question?
- Are there aspects of the organization's culture that will affect whether the project is a success?
- Who are the formal and informal decision makers in the organization who could influence the project's success?

Let's go back to our slightly silly example of how you are going to get to your aunt's funeral. The general question seems to be how you are going to get to 80 miles from Casper, preferably by tomorrow night. This is the primary problem, but a variety of related questions also need to be answered. For example, what airlines fly into Casper? When do they fly from Dallas to Casper? How about trains? Can you rent a car in Casper? How long would it take to drive there from Dallas? Note that the initial problem or initial question becomes more complicated as you start to think more deeply about it.

Now let's look at a more serious example. XtraComfort is a shoe manufacturer, well known for making very comfortable shoes (we also refer to this company in a later chapter of this book). The company has traditionally sold its shoes in several large department stores as well as in independent shoe stores. Recently, a number of shoe stores have begun selling online. One of the many brands some of them offer, albeit in a limited selection of styles and sizes, is XtraComfort.

The advent of retail sales on the Internet has raised the question within XtraComfort of whether the company should set up its own online retail business to sell XtraComfort—and only XtraComfort—shoes. To help answer this question, the company contracted with a marketing consulting firm that specializes in online retail sales.

At one level, the question posed to the consultants was fairly simple: Should XtraComfort set up an online retail store to sell XtraComfort shoes? However, the company is not merely interested is getting a simple yes-or-no answer. In fact, there are several questions that need to be answered, and they are fairly complex. For example, one question the company is concerned about is the cost to set up and maintain an online store. The company also wants to know how profitable such a store is likely to be and how quickly XtraComfort is likely to realize its return on investment. Other questions are of concern as well: Is opening an online store likely to result in an increase in sales of XtraComfort shoes overall, or will sales be flat as some customers began buying online instead of in department stores? How would the online store affect XtraComfort's relations with current distributors? XtraComfort has an agreement with a large department store chain, allowing it to distribute certain XtraComfort shoes in their stores exclusively. Will the chain accuse XtraComfort of undercutting the department store's sales by selling online?

You probably could think of several other questions that the managers at XtraComfort would want to explore before deciding whether to open a retail business on the Internet. The point is that there are usually no simple questions in the consulting business. Consultants often need to spend considerable time exploring what the client wants to find out and why finding this out is important. Much of this discussion should occur during the contract phase, as discussed in chapter 3; however, this discussion needs to be continued to ensure that you are addressing the correct question and, furthermore, that it is being addressed at the depth that is necessary.

Another advantage of having extended discussions with the primary contact at the client company, and perhaps with other members of the organization as well, is that there may be hidden problems that need to be uncovered if the consultant is to answer the question the client has posed.

Our next example involves a problem confronting the Department of Children's and Family Services, a large government agency. Among this agency's responsibilities is placing children who are wards of the state in foster homes and, subsequently, monitoring their health and safety. Unfortunately, the agency has been under attack recently following the death of a child who was neglected while in foster care. Among the criticisms hurled at the agency was that it "lost" several children in its care.

The director of the agency hired a team of consultants to offer recommendations on how to correct some of its problems. In particular, the director asked the consultants to focus on the training the caseworkers received and on their time-management skills. Among the apparent problems was that the workers received very little training for what appeared to be a very complex and frustrating job. The director believed that the lack of training was the cause of the workers "losing" children in the system.

As the first step in the data collection process, the consultants interviewed several caseworkers and supervisors. On the basis of these interviews, the consultants determined that the system for tracking and monitoring children in foster care seemed to be seriously flawed. So, following up on this initial diagnosis, the consultants broadened their inquiry to include the foster care system, as well as the selection process and training of caseworkers.

After gathering the relevant data, the consultants concluded that the computer system used for tracking the children was flawed and was responsible for most of the problems of "losing" children. They proposed that a new system be developed to provide more effective tracking and monitoring of the children.

Although it was true that the process for selecting and training the caseworkers needed to be improved, the caseworkers could never have performed their jobs effectively, regardless of how well trained they were, because the tracking and monitoring system was so inadequate. If the consultants had focused on finding problems in the selection and training system, as the director suggested they should, then the consultants would have recommended a lot of so-called improvements, but the children would have remained at risk. In short, the consultants would have been focusing on the wrong problem.

As this example illustrates, serious effort has to go into defining and diagnosing an organizational problem. Even in our original silly example, you might have been focusing on the wrong problem. Perhaps the first problem you needed to address, before determining how to get to the funeral, was whether the information your mother gave you was accurate. Maybe your aunt really isn't dead. Or maybe the funeral isn't in Casper but Chicago. After all, your mother is sometimes as daffy as your aunt. A savvy consultant recognizes that what the client has identified as the problem may not be the problem at all but a symptom of another problem entirely.

As should be obvious by now, like icebergs (see Fig. 4.1), 90% of which are not visible to the naked eye, problems in organizations are often neither visible nor understood by clients or others in the organizations. That which can be seen is much easier to manage and change: job descriptions, personnel policies, missions/goals, and so forth. That which cannot be seen is much more difficult to manage and change because, much like an iceberg, the problems remain under the surface. Thus, problems in the informal organization (e.g., group sentiments and norms, employees' emotions, power relationships) are much more difficult to identify and change. Consequently, it is extremely important for consultants to obtain as much background information about what the client has said is the organization's problem as well as the symptoms or behaviors the client has identified. This process of uncovering the real problems in an organization is often known as conducting a situation analysis.

FIG. 4.1.   The organizational "iceberg."

Although one can never be totally certain of identifying the real problem, there are several things you can do to increase the probability of focusing on the real problem rather than on just one of possibly many symptoms. This moves us to the next step: determining the information needed to solve the problem.

DETERMINING WHAT INFORMATION IS NEEDED

Once you have defined the problem to your and your client's satisfaction and are fairly certain what questions need to be answered, the next step is to decide what information is needed to answer those questions. In most cases, the information will be fairly obvious from the questions asked.

In our example of needing to get from Dallas to Casper, and assuming that you have confirmed that the information your mother has given you is correct, your key questions should focus on your options in transportation. Which airlines fly into Casper? At what times? Can you rent a car there? Is your aunt's town accessible by car, or do you need to rent a mule? These questions define what information is needed. A very efficient method for progressing is to make a list of the information you need, find out where you can get the information (the next step), and then collect the information (Step 4).

Once you have devised a clear problem statement or research question, data collection should proceed efficiently. For this reason, we recommend forcing yourself to state the research question in writing, being as clear as possible about the problem. Next, prepare a list of questions that need to be answered and then decide what information is needed to answer those questions.

Let's assume for a minute that you have been retained to assess why a firm's new advertising strategy has been ineffective in increasing sales. As stated here, this problem is too broad to investigate or to devise a data collection strategy. You might begin by interviewing a few people in the advertising unit—that is, conducting a situation analysis. This might lead to consideration of the advertising campaign itself, which you might conclude was unsuccessful. On the basis of information gleaned from the interviews, you might then conclude that you really need to answer the following series of questions:

- Has anything happened internally or externally that might have adversely affected the advertising campaign (e.g., change in key personnel, change in economic climate for the company's product)?
- Have sales really been lower? (Perhaps there has been a change in the accounting system that has affected how sales are recorded.)
- Has production kept up with demand for the product?

- Have customer complaints and returned product accounted for lost revenue?

The point is that the advertising campaign may have been successful, but other parts of the organization may have been unable to support the campaign's results.

Developed carefully, research questions such as the ones just listed can be extremely useful in understanding a problem affecting an organization, what questions need to be answered, and what information needs to be obtained to answer these questions. With that focus, you can then begin developing a data collection strategy.

DETERMINING SOURCES OF THE INFORMATION

The next step is to determine who has the information you need to answer your and the client's questions and how you can get the answers these questions. In the example of needing to get from Dallas to Casper, you might want to find out which airlines fly to Casper and their flight schedules. Where can you get that information? One option would be to call every airline you know. That sounds very time consuming, however. Maybe a better idea is to call a travel agent, who can access the information almost immediately and figure out how many stopovers or plane changes the trip would involve. The travel agent might even be able to recommend alternative routes, such as flying into Denver and renting a car and driving from there. You might also want to look at an Internet site that specializes in travel, such as Orbitz or Travelocity.

Determining where to access information can often be rather difficult. To illustrate our point here, let's look again at the case of XtraComfort Shoes. One of the questions the company wanted answered was whether an online retail store would be profitable and, if so, about how much profit XtraComfort could expect it to make and how long it would take the company to realize a return on its investment (if ever). XtraComfort also wanted to know how setting up an online store would affect the company's relationships with its current distributors. These are very tough questions. Moreover, the client wants hard data to back up whatever conclusions the consultants reach. In this case, the data collection phase is made even more difficult when the consultant is trying to predict future events.

COLLECTING THE DATA

Once you have a good idea of the information you need to address the issue of interest to the client and know where it might be obtained, the next step (Step 4 in our model) is to decide how to collect the information. Before we begin describing some of the formal methods associated with collecting data, we want to remind you that every interaction you have in the organization is an opportunity to observe and collect data. As Stroh and Johnson noted in the "From the Experts" section for this chapter, data collection begins the moment you make any initial contact in the organization. Observing the person's attitude about the organization for which he or she works, how the person speaks about and refers to employees, and whether "what the organization says" matches "what it actually does" can sometimes provide more useful information than you can gather from sur-

---

From the Experts ...
Data Collection Begins at the Beginning!
by Linda Stroh and Homer Johnson, Professors, HRIR, Graduate School of Business, Loyola University Chicago

Many consultants think that the data collection stage of a project begins after the proposal is written and the contract is agreed on. It has been our experience that data collection begins much sooner—the moment you meet or speak with a potential client. Observing the person's attitude about the organization he or she works for, how the person speaks about and refers to employees, and whether "what the organization says" matches "what it actually does" can sometimes provide more useful information than you can gather from surveys and interviews. For example, one pharmaceutical company with which we worked was interested in shortening the time that it took between their idea to develop a new product and the actual launching of that product.

Our major area of interest for this project was the research design team. The top-level managers claimed this research design group was the most important in the organization—according to these top managers, without the research design team, there was no organization. Yet, before we had even written our proposal to do the project, it became clear through casual observation that the company's research development team was not the most respected or most highly rewarded group after all. The walls of the company's hallways were filled with photographs of top salespeople and marketing and promotional materials; there were no visible signs that there even was a research and development team.

Furthermore, in conversation, when we casually asked who were the most highly compensated executives in the company, members of research and development were never mentioned. And even before meeting with our contact person at the organization, we noticed by looking at the organizational chart—we're sure you've already guessed it—that were no top-level research people on the most senior team.

So, before we even began writing our proposal or formally collecting data, we had already collected some very useful information. Thus, it is our belief that collecting data begins at the very beginning of a project. Don't wait for formal data collection phase to start observing the organization. If we had, we could have missed out on some very valuable data!

veys and interviews. We encourage you to use every opportunity and interaction to observe the behaviors in the organization and keep careful records of these observations.

Next, this section provides a cursory review of four common ways to collect data: (a) conducting interviews, (b) performing surveys, (c) observing, and (d) reviewing existing records. About 90% of the time, consultants use one of these techniques. The purpose of this section is to give you some indication of how each of these techniques are used and the advantages and disadvantages of each.

Probably the most important rule when it comes to data collection is that the collection technique should produce the information you need to answer the question posed by the client. Thus, you always start by determining *what* information is needed, *where* the information is available or who has that information and, finally, *which* technique to use that will best uncover that information. Although some consultants specialize in one of these four techniques, the problem should dictate the technique you use, not whether you prefer one technique over another. Many consultants end up using a combination of techniques, often called *data triangulation*, which affords them an even broader perspective on the issue.

Interviews: Individuals and Group

Consultants usually find out quickly that interviews provide the foundation for their work. Here, we touch only briefly on a few of the basics of this extremely important data collection method. Chapter 5 is devoted exclusively to helping you develop your skills as an interviewer. It is essential that you learn the basics and practice interviewing as much as possible.

Interviews are fairly time consuming and, because time is money, they can be somewhat costly. However, they are one of the best and most frequently used ways to gain information. Their great advantage is that they enable you to probe deeply and therefore gain a good understanding of an issue. Say, for example, that during an interview a customer expresses dissatisfaction with a particular product. The interviewer has the luxury of following up and ask why the customer feels this way, something that is very difficult to do in a questionnaire. Let's say the customer then says that the product is hard to handle. The interviewer might then ask "How is it hard to handle? In what way?" The customer might then respond "Because the grip is in an awkward position." The interviewer might then ask the customer to demonstrate the problem. By the end of the interview, the consultant will have gained a pretty good understanding of the customer's concerns and have some good ideas about how to redesign the product to address these concerns. The opportunity to probe deeply, to follow up on comments, and to discover causes are what make the interview such a valuable way to elicit information.

Interviews are typically conducted in one of three formats: (a) face to face, (b) in a focus group, or (c) by telephone. Although they take time, interviews are critical when your goal is to help a group learn about itself and how effectively it is working.

In chapter 5 we provide more information about interview techniques, but the following are just a few pieces of advice that are especially important when conducting interviews in work organizations:

- Try to maintain objectivity and consistency from one interview to the next.
- Consider using a prepared script and taking notes.
- Schedule your time carefully. Conducting interviews back to back can be tiring and confusing.
- Assure interviewees that their names will not be attached to the information; interviewees are often fearful about losing their job if they say something negative.
- Probe, ask why, and probe some more, to get at the underlying causes of a problem or issue.

Surveys or Questionnaires

Like interviews, a survey or questionnaire can be a very effective tool for learning about how the people in an organization feel about a variety of issues, from the way management treats employees; to whether employees receive adequate, valuable training; to whether decision making proceeds in a top-down or bottom-up manner. Surveys are also used extensively for conducting market research and for assessing customer and patient satisfaction. One of the attractions of conducting a survey is that the results can be easily converted into hard numbers ("87% of our customers indicated that they are generally or very satisfied with our service") and comparisons made across time periods ("This is a 4% increase over the rate recorded last year at this time").

Questionnaires are especially useful if you need to obtain information from a large number of people or a group in which the people are widely dispersed. For example, suppose management at an automobile assembly plant wants to know the level of job satisfaction among the company's 3,000 workers, as well as their reactions to some recent changes in work rules.

One option would be to try to interview all 3,000 employees, or perhaps even a sample of 300; however, doing all those interviews (even 300) would entail considerable time and expense. A much quicker and less expensive approach would be to design a short questionnaire consisting of multiple-choice questions, which are easily scored by computer. The questionnaire could be administered to some or all employees in a day or two, and a data summary could be tabulated in another couple of days. Thus, data collection and analysis would be both quick and inexpensive.

The advantage of conducting a survey can also be a disadvantage, however, in that multiple-choice questions often do not reveal the underlying reasons people responded as they did. For example, suppose the automobile supply company administered a job satisfaction questionnaire to all 3,000 employees. Some of the questions focused on the employees' reactions to the recent changes in the work rules, in particular to how employees are assigned to work teams. One possible question could be "How satisfied are you with the new system of assigning employees to work teams?" The respondent would be then be asked to check one of four responses: "very satisfied," "generally satisfied," "generally dissatisfied," or "very dissatisfied." If most of the respondents checked "very satisfied" or "generally satisfied," then interpreting the results would be fairly easy, or at least the company would know that the employees were not pushing for a change in that policy. But what if most of the respondents said they were dissatisfied with the new system? Then the question becomes: Why? What parts of the system do they not like? A good interviewer would have probed to answer this question; in a survey, this is rarely done. In other words, although the survey conducted for the automobile supply company provided a quick read on employee satisfaction, it raised an additional question that needs to be answered: Why is the level of dissatisfaction so high?

Theoretically, the consultant could have added an open-ended question that said something to the effect of "If you responded that you are generally or very dissatisfied with the new system for assigning employees to work teams, please explain below why you are dissatisfied and what changes you would like the company to make." However, then someone would have had to read, interpret, and summarize all those responses. This too can be very time consuming and costly, particularly if a large number of employees are being surveyed and the questionnaire contains many open-ended questions. So this raises a dilemma: How much and what do you include in a questionnaire?

Regardless of the organization or issue being investigated, developing a questionnaire that provides accurate and consistent results is a well-honed skill. Most important, you need to be sure that the questions will yield the information being sought. All too often, survey questions are ambiguous or confusing. One way to avoid this problem is to pilot test a survey with several people before administering it to a large group.

The following are a few other guidelines for developing surveys.

Choosing the Sample. Obviously, the first concern in picking a sample of people to survey is that they must be able to provide the information you need to address the issue the client wants answered. It is always best to use a sample that is both large and representative of the organization or the customer base in terms of age, gender, department breakdown, and so on.

Administering the Survey. Surveys can be administered on site, mailed to respondents, or given to respondents to take home and return or mail back. An increasing number of surveys are sent to respondents by e-mail, although confidentiality may not be guaranteed. As with other decisions, you and the client need to decide together whether it would be best to mail the questionnaires to employees at home, e-mail them to a work address, or distribute and administer them in so other way. Many surveys are now administered online. The respondent is directed to a Web site, provided an entry code for a questionnaire, asked to complete the survey, and then send it back. The results are tabulated instantaneously. Regardless of how the survey is administered, the first page needs to explain why the survey is being conducted, that it is supported by the client organization, and that all replies will remain totally confidential.

You will want to consider the following as you develop the items for the questionnaire:

- Do the questions lead to responses that address your research question?
- In what order should the questions be asked? (An answer to one question may influence how someone responds to another question.)
- Are questions phrased as simply and straightforwardly as possible?
- Are questions objective? Respondents should not be led to answers.
- Are the questions as clear and concise as possible?
- Should a pretest be conducted on a small but representative sample?

Direct Observation

Observing people while they work, or in other settings, such as while they are making purchase decisions, is another way that consultants gather data. The advantage of this technique is that people are observed (usually) in their natural setting, doing what they normally do. This is in contrast to the interview or survey, in which people report on how they feel or behave. We know that what people say they do is sometimes different from what they actually do. This does not mean they are lying (although they may be) but rather is a reminder that people often are not totally aware of the details of their behavior.

Although direct observation has certain advantages, one possible drawback is that people sometimes react differently than they normally would when they are aware that they are being observed—in other words, the knowledge that they are being watched changes their behavior. For example, a consultant observing workers on an assembly line might think they are consistently cautious about safety and quality issues. What the consultant does not realize, however, is that when he or she is not around, the employees use a shortcut on the line that could put safety and quality at risk.

This disadvantage of direct observation can usually be overcome by being as unobtrusive as possible and careful not to interfere in any way with the action taking place. The goal is not to affect or manipulate the situation in any way but simply to record what is happening, being careful to be as objective and consistent across observations as possible.

Most of the time, people being observed will, over time, become comfortable and behave as they would if the consultant were not observing them. For example, a consultant who was asked to investigate the causes of conflict among members of a management team asked to sit in on their management meetings. At the beginning of the first meeting, the members of the team were on their very best behavior and models of civility and cooperation. About an hour later, however, a couple of rather nasty conflicts ensued, which team members later told the consultant was typical of what occurs in their meetings. It took the team about an hour to become comfortable with the consultant being present, and after that they behaved as if she were not even there.

One of the questions that needs to be resolved before observing people in the workplace is when to observe. In the case described earlier, for example, an astute consultant might have wondered whether the employees in the automobile plant behaved differently when the line was moving quickly and pressure was high than they did when production was slow. It behooved the consultant to make sure he observed (i.e., sampled behavior) under both conditions.

Several variations are possible regarding the use of the observation technique. For example, videotaping has become more common. The obvious advantage is that videotape provides a permanent record of behavior and can be replayed repeatedly for analysis by the consultant and perhaps even by the person or group being observed.

Other consultants have people work in, or make decisions in, special rooms and observe their behavior there. Some consultants combine both observation techniques with personal interviews. For example, a consultant hired to improve a company sales techniques followed its top salespeople, observed (and took notes on) their sales approach, and later interviewed them to find out what they were thinking as they worked, why they asked certain questions, and why they made certain comments.

Here are a few general guidelines to bear in mind if you do direct observations:

- Decide before the observation what you want to focus on. What specific behavior is of interest or concern? Employees' actions and interactions? Spatial and temporal patterns? Social interactions?
- Design and use a checklist to remind you what you want to learn about the situation you are observing, but be flexible—and add new items as needed.
- Be as unobtrusive as possible. Do not interfere in any way with the event being observed.
- Make sure you observe at different times and under different conditions, particularly if you have reason to believe that subjects' behavior may change under different conditions .

Reviewing Existing Records

Most organizations collect volumes of internal information, which, given the availability of electronic data processing, is usually easily accessible. Under federal and state law, some of this information is required to be available to the public. For example, public corporations are required to make available vast amounts of financial data every quarter. Likewise, company safety and health records are available through the Occupational Safety and Health Administration. Company data on hiring and terminations, employee head counts, pay, gender, race, and so on, are also available, from the U.S. Department of Labor and other agencies. Finally, many businesses have extensive records on sales, returns, and customer complaints that they share with consultants.

In addition to data that are available to the general public, other data are available for purchase from research groups. The problem for the consultant is not that there is not enough information but how to sift through the volumes that exist.

We recommend that you begin by asking yourself the first three questions of the five-step model: What's the problem? What information do I need? Who has it, or where is it?

Let's look in a little more detail at some of the data collection possibilities in existing records:

Internal Records.   As noted earlier, most companies generate a wide variety of information, much of which you would have access to if you were consulting for the company. Gaining access to this information is much easier since the advent of enterprisewide software. Records of financial data, for example, are among the most complete, because it is critical that companies know how well they are doing financially and because publicly held companies are required to make financial information available to the general public.

Sales information also is readily available; however, although a company may have good records on how much product it sells each month, it may take some digging to find out what individual customers purchased as well as the sales revenue for individual products.

We will not attempt to describe all the information available from internal company records but offer you a bit of a warning: You cannot always assume that company records are accurate. Accidents, as just one example, are often underreported. Supervisors are sometimes reluctant to report injuries because they think it will reflect negatively on their performance and result in increases in the company's insurance rates.

Other information may be inaccurate as well, as highlighted in a recent scandal in which several newspapers were found to have inflated their circulation figures. In this case the higher (and false) circulation figures allowed the newspaper to charge their advertisers considerably more, because advertising rates are based on circulation rates.

The point here is that you should not assume that information is necessarily accurate just because it is in "official" company records. The information could have been recorded inaccurately, or someone could have deliberately lied.

Public Records.   Much of the information organizations provide to federal and state government agencies is available to the public, although the record may or may identify companies by name. Certainly in the case of an annual report, you will, of course, know to which company the data pertain. Other publications, however, such as those produced by the U.S. Department of Labor, include averages—of annual salaries for various categories of workers, for example—based on information companies provide but do not identify what any one company pays its workers.

Census data can also be invaluable to consultants. Suppose a major high-end retailer—for example, Nordstrom or Lord & Taylor—has contracted with you to help decide where to open several new stores. Where would you start with your research?

One possibility would be to get in your car and drive around the United States, or maybe even in Europe. However, that would be a huge waste of time and, more important, would not give you the information you are looking for. One piece of information that would be helpful is that high-end retailers target customers with very specific demographics. The easiest way to gain access to this information is through the U.S. Bureau of the Census, which collects and distributes demographic information free to anyone interested in obtaining it. Information is available on population density and on the populations in different areas; on the average income of people living in these areas, on the number of children in the families in these areas, on the level of education of the people living there, and on their ages, gender, ethnicity, and numerous other aspects of their lives that would be extremely helpful in identifying choice sites for expansion. Moreover, this information is easily accessible at no cost.

Reviewing census data would help you narrow the list of choice store sites considerably. But wait—more valuable, easy-to-access information is out there. If you are a good researcher, you will want to evaluate accessibility to transportation for each of the sites under consideration. One source to which you would want to refer are area maps, available online, that indicate all the highways and other roads in an area. If you are interested in what other retailers are in the area, you can check out the online Yellow Pages. Taxes? The tax structure, local and state, should be posted online as well. Zoning restrictions? Again, state and local governments have all this. Cost of land? Same.

We could go on, but the point is that existing public records are a great resource for consultants. Most of the information is free, and it is all very easily accessible.

Other Records.   Many sources of private information are available to consultants. You may sometimes have to pay a fee.

One source of private information is private research companies, many of which regularly collect information on specific industries or issues. For example, volumes of data are available on the automobile industry, ranging from sales per car model, defects per car model, customer complaints per car model, who purchases what model, how many people will purchase a new car next year, and so on. Much of this information is available for purchase.

Another good source of information is professional associations, which regularly conduct studies of interest to their members. Much of this information is available free of charge (or for a minimal fee) to the organizations' members. As just one example, some of these associations collect salary and benefits information for major cities or regions of the United States. Information is also available on such matters as the average salaries for various categories of employees, benefits offered, and average salary increases. Some organizations also collect information on how many employees the companies in various areas intend to hire in the coming year. Obviously, this information is of great value in determining salaries to offer as well as salary increases companies should consider offering to reduce turnover and stay competitive.

PROS AND CONS OF EACH METHOD

As should be obvious from the preceding discussion, each data collection method has advantages and disadvantages. The first consideration in deciding which method to use is which one will yield the information you need to answer the question as simply as possible. Beyond that, you should be aware of the potential problems you encounter using each technique. A summary of the advantages and disadvantages of each method we have highlighted is provided in Table 4.2.

REAL-LIFE EXAMPLES

In the following section, we discuss consulting projects that have actually been undertaken. As you review each problem the consultant was asked to solve, ask yourself the following questions: What is the purpose of the proposed assessment/study? What is the problem? What information is needed to solve this problem? Finally, how would you collect the data that are needed? Decide for yourself which data collection methods would be most appropriate before reading what the consultant did in each case.

TABLE 4.2
Advantages and Disadvantages of Major Data Collection Methods

Method	Advantages	Disadvantages
Interview	Flexibility Can elicit in-depth information Can observe body language	Interviewer bias Socially acceptable replies Time consuming/expensive
Survey	Easy to get data on large numbers of people Easy to quantify Cost effective Easy to compare and contrast	Limited to questions as asked Respondent error No follow-up Difficult to assign meaning
Direct observation	Hands-on experience Observe actual behavior Immediate results Flexible	Observer bias Difficult to assign meaning Participant awareness of observation Expensive
Records	Provide relevant background information Little cost Minimal bias	Time consuming May not have needed data Difficult to interpret

The Case of the Business Travelers

A major hotel chain wanted to more directly target business travelers, so it instituted several changes designed to attract these guests. For example, guests can now register by cell phone on the way to the hotel, and the bell captain will have the room key ready when the customer arrives. The hotel also provides free Internet service, free photocopy service, and a variety of other amenities. The hotel marketing department was eager to determine whether business travelers liked these services as well as what other services they wanted at the chain's hotels.

To gather this information, the hotel left a short questionnaire in each room. Unfortunately, very few questionnaires were ever returned. Next, the hotel offered a coupon for a free drink at the hotel bar for anyone who turned in the questionnaire. Again, very few people responded. Reaching the point of desperation, the hotel hired a consultant to design a strategy to help get the information the hotel wanted. What data collection technique should the consultant use? Why didn't the in-room questionnaires elicit much of a response?

In this case, the consultant recommended two approaches. First, she suggested that the hotel conduct focus groups with business travelers to determine what services that wanted and, if they were familiar with the hotel in question, to evaluate the current services. Second, she suggested that the hotel conduct a very brief phone survey of business guests to learn their experiences at the hotel and how their stay could have been more enjoyable. The survey would be conducted on a regular basis, enabling the hotel to track its progress in improving its business guests' satisfaction. In addition, the consultant monitored the number of business guests who stayed in the hotel chain each month and the number of nights they stayed.

Why had the in-room questionnaire not provided the information the hotel needed? First and foremost, business travelers are usually rushed at checkout time, and filling out a questionnaire is one of the last things they want to think about. The offer of a free drink did not work as an incentive mainly because most guests didn't see it as an incentive, as they were given their coupon for their drink on their way out of the hotel, often at 8:00 in the morning.

The Case of the Salary Policy Problem

In a later chapter, you will read about an organization that recently went through a restructuring. Afterwards, the company asked some consultants to interview employees to determine what issues related to restructuring were still unresolved. Some employees reported dissatisfaction with how salaries were being determined for new employees. Some new employees were being paid more to perform the same or similar tasks as older employees. The board of directors asked the consultants to explore whether the complaints were valid.

What information should a consultant seek out? What data-gathering method should he or she use?

The consultant wanted to verify that there was in fact a discrepancy in what new hires and current employees in similar jobs were being paid, so she examined the company records on the new hires for the past 2 years, noting their job category, experience, education, and starting salaries. She also compared the salary policy that was in effect before the restructuring with the policy in effect since the restructuring. She concluded that the new salary policy was appropriate but that two units were still following the old policy. The board and the director corrected the discrepancies in those units.

The Case of the Reluctant Managers

A major multinational company was having problems finding enough talented managers to fill key positions in their international subsidiaries. Unlike the situation in previous years, employees were turning down international career opportunities. Sending employees abroad has been an extremely effective way to incorporate new technologies in foreign operations, improve communication between the foreign subsidiaries and the home office, and provide developmental leadership opportunities for key managers. Given that these assignments were highly important to the strategic mission of the company, the company was eager to find out why managers were no longer accepting these assignments. For this project, a good way for a consultant to begin is by interviewing managers who have turned down international assignments in the past 2 years. The consultant could also interview managers who have returned from international assignments and compare the responses of each. You might also conduct telephone or e-mail surveys of managers who are currently on assignments overseas.

The Case of the Lean Manufacturing Company

An international manufacturing company with plants throughout the world embarked on an initiative to institute lean manufacturing and Six Sigma quality techniques in its facilities. In a train-the-trainer program, managers from each facility were trained and, in turn, they trained managers and employees in their facilities. One concern, however, was whether the training was being conducted correctly. Some consultants were hired to explore this issue. What would you recommend they do?

The consultants in this case traveled to each facility and directly observed training sessions. They also observed the Six Sigma groups in action. Each facility was asked to document its efforts concerning this initiative as well as the results obtained. Approximately 1 year after the training, a group of managers and consultants from corporate headquarters visited each facility and spent 3 days observing the Six Sigma groups in action as well as reviewing the progress in quality improvement in that facility.

A Case of Sexual Harassment

A woman, who claims to represent several other women in her work unit, has complained to the human resources manager that their (male) supervisor frequently tells offensive jokes, makes references to their breasts and bodies, and shows them photos of nude women from a magazine to which he subscribes. She claims that the women have told him that they find his behavior offensive; however, he just laughs and tells them that they need to "loosen up." One of the company's internal human resources consultants was assigned to review the case. How would he or she start? What data collection method would be most efficient?

The consultant began by interviewing the women who were reportedly the targets of the offensive behavior and documented in some detail what happened, including the frequency of the incidents. Other employees in the unit were also interviewed to determine what they had observed. Finally, the supervisor was interviewed. He admitted to many of the behaviors that the women complained about. However, he claimed that he was just "joking around" and that the women were being overly sensitive.

The Case of the Slow Fast-Service Company

The competition between office supply distributors in a major metropolitan area had become very intense, particularly since the arrival of Office Max and other discount supply stores. One of the long-time distributors realized that it would have to change its marketing strategy to survive and developed a next-day delivery service. If a customer phones in a supply order by 2:00 p.m., the order is delivered the next morning. Although this strategy appeared to be sound, based on the number of customers who signed up for the service, execution was a problem. The company was plagued by orders being lost; orders being delivered incomplete; and orders taking 2 or more days, instead of overnight, to deliver. The company has hired some consultants to find out why so many problems have been occurring. How would they begin with the process of data collection?

The consultants started by attempting to understand the next-day delivery system, beginning with the point when an order was phoned in and ending when the order was delivered. Having mapped the process, the consultants then traced several orders through the system to determine at which points the system was working well and where the problems were occurring. It appeared that the crux of the problem was at one point in the system, when the orders were being put together in the warehouse. Subsequently, the system was changed to correct this problem.

The Case of the Start-Up

A new debt-reduction company in the San Francisco Bay area had undergone extensive growth. The company, started by two partners (Brad and Andrew), had opened its doors just 18 months ago. The partners had started out with a sincere interest in building a culture that would be so attractive that even they would want to work for the company. Today, the company has more than $5 million in revenues, 100 employees, and offices in five locations. Brad and Andrew want to maintain the employee-friendly environment, but they are afraid of losing touch with their employees as the company becomes larger. Specifically, the partners want a system in place so that they monitor whether the company is attracting and retaining talented employees.

The consultant began by conducting a job satisfaction survey, which was developed with the help of the client's top managers. The company also wanted a system in place to monitor overall job satisfaction once a year. The final questionnaire consisted of 20 questions that employees would be asked every year plus 10 that could be revised as necessary. A Web site was set up to administer the survey, and each employee was given a code number to enter the site. Employees were asked to complete the questionnaire within a 5-day period, and results were available within another week.

Although collecting data is often a formal process, it is also important to remember that every interaction with someone in the client company is an opportunity to collect information. For example, you can learn a lot from observing how the organization treats employees. Also observe how conflicts are handled: Does the person in power control the decision-making process, or do others have a fair say in decision making? Is the culture inclusive, or are there subgroups that have little or no power? Observing how power and status are handled can be very useful in understanding an organization. Just remember to focus as much as possible on behavior related to your research question.

By reading this chapter, we hope you have gained insight into the data collection process and, more specifically, into the first four steps of the diagnosis and data collection model. In chapter 5 we provide more information on the interview process. We will then turn to Step 5 of the model as we focus on drawing conclusions based on the information you have collected.

SUMMARY

In this chapter we have provided a step-by-step process for developing a project strategy and action plan. We emphasized the importance to the success of a project of accurately diagnosing problems and collecting appropriate data. This process begins with defining the problem or issue, deciding what information you need to collect and where to find it, and determining the best method to use to collect that information. Also emphasized was the importance of identifying and solving the real problem, as opposed to merely a symptom of the problem.

The four most frequently used methods of data collection—interviews, surveys, direct observation, and reviewing existing records—were each described, and cases that exemplify when to use each method were provided. The next section lists the key success factors that define this phase of developing a project strategy and collecting data successfully.

KEY SUCCESS FACTORS FOR DEVELOPING A PROJECT STRATEGY

- Define the problem thoroughly and deeply.
- Be sure you are solving the real problem, not just the problem as stated by the client or identified in your proposal.
- Recognize that collecting data is both a formal and an informal process that encompasses not only interviews, surveys, and so forth, but also observing interactions in the organization.
- Clearly define what questions need to be answered and what information is needed to answer those questions.
- Determine who has the necessary information and where it can be obtained.
- Choose the most effective data collection technique that will enable you to access the information that is needed. If possible, use methods that are relatively quick and inexpensive.
- Recognize that every interaction you have within the organization is one in which you are collecting data.

5

Interviewing

One of the most basic and important data collection skills consultants should have in their toolkit is knowing how to be a good interviewer. Interviewing skills are used at all stages of a consulting project: from the first meeting with a prospective client, through diagnosis of the problem and action, to successful completion of the project. Good interviewing skills can yield valuable insights and information.

Consultants need valid and useful information on which to base decisions and to assist clients in making decisions. Interviews are one way to gather this information, whether the focus is the client's expectations for a project, problems the client or a unit of an organization is facing, or employees' or customers' perceptions of a specific issue.

Interviews also offer opportunities to establish positive relationships based on openness and trust. For this reason, interviews can lay the foundation for establishing trusting, caring relationships between consultant and clients.

Interviewing is a special skill that differs significantly from ordinary conversation. In most ordinary conversations involving two people, the focus is on neutral topics: the weather, your vacation trip, the new car you bought, or the cute thing your child said, to name just a few examples. Ordinary conversations tend to veer away from controversial issues, such as religion and politics, and stay at a surface level. In a consulting interview, the goal is just the opposite: to get below the surface, to get beyond what it is socially desirable to talk about, and delve into issues that are sometimes sensitive and often controversial. Unlike many ordinary conversations, an interview is serious and purposeful.

Each interview should have a clear, specific goal, which you should usually clarify before the interview begins. You should also have a plan—based on the information that needs to be gathered. Keeping this information in mind, you can devise a set of questions to achieve the desired outcome.

To conduct a successful interview takes considerable preparation and skill. This chapter covers some of the fundamentals of how to become an effective interviewer.

THE INTERVIEW SETTING

Choosing an appropriate setting in which to conduct an interview is important to its success. Too often, consultants conduct interviews in a company cafeteria, in a hallway, or on a noisy factory floor. These settings often lead to poor interviews, as both parties can be easily distracted, may have difficulty hearing each other, and may feel physically uncomfortable. To maximize the chances of success, interviews should ideally be conducted in settings that are:

- Quiet
- Free of distractions
- Private (no one will be able to hear or observe the interview as it is taking place)
- Furnished with comfortable seating

In addition, there should be a table or chairs so that you can face the interviewee, establish eye contact, and observe the interviewee's facial and body reactions.

The importance of choosing a comfortable, private place in which to conduct interviews cannot be overemphasized. In the recent U.S. presidential elections, many commentators, including Tim Russert of NBC News, were criticized for interviewing the candidates in uncomfortable, contrived-looking settings. For the Russert interview, the President and Russert were seated in uncomfortable seats facing in awkward positions, forcing contrived postures for both. Thus, to some, the whole interview appeared strained. Consultants frequently ask to have an empty office or room reserved exclusively for them to conduct interviews. If you are interviewing someone in his or her own office, ask the person to close the door and put the phone on hold so you can talk without being interrupted.

BODY LANGUAGE: A REFLECTION OF ATTITUDE

Another key component to consider when conducting interviews is your body language, which can say a lot about your attitude toward the person you are interviewing. Ideally, you want to let the interviewee feel that you are interested in the information and ideas expressed. If the interviewee thinks you are interested in what is being said, then he or she is far more likely to be cooperative and to volunteer information. If the interviewee thinks you are not interested, then he or she is likely to feel very little reason to cooperate.

Your body language is one of the most obvious ways that you communicate interest—or lack of interest—in the person you are interviewing. The rules for communicating this interest are really quite simple and easy to follow:

- Face the interviewee so that both of you can observe each other's reactions. Sitting at a slight angle (45 degrees), rather than directly in front of the person, may make him or her more comfortable.
- Make frequent eye contact, but don't stare. Also avoid staring out the window, at the wall, or at notes. Occasional eye contact signals interest in what the interviewee is saying and is a way to pick up on the interviewee's facial expressions as he or she is talking.
- Sit upright in your seat, and lean slightly forward, toward the interviewee.
- Signal you are paying attention by nodding in response to comments and/or by saying "I understand" or "I see" to indicate that the message is being received. Asking for clarification of a point or summarizing a point after the interviewee says something is another way to signal you are paying attention.
- Finally, taking notes indicates to the interviewee that his or her opinions are important. These notes will also be useful if you have to summarize data from a series of interviews in a report. Be careful, however, that note-taking does not become a distraction but rather is an integral part of the interview process.

GENERAL RULES

By following some other general rules of interviewing, you are likely to elicit valuable information from your interviewees while ensuring that they feel comfortable and at ease as you ask them questions. These rules are summarized in Table 5.1.

Clarify the Purpose

All interviews have a purpose, even those in which you are fishing for ideas. Make sure you are clear as to the purpose of the interview. Why are you conducting it? What outcomes are you hoping for? Once you are clear about the purpose, ask yourself: What do I need to accomplish for

TABLE 5.1
General Rules for Interviewing

- Be clear about what information you want to elicit—that is, the purpose of the interview.
- Prepare questions in advance.
- Design the interview for the time available.
- Keep the interview focused.
- Stay flexible.
- Maintain a bias-free and politically neutral stance.
- Ask one question at time.
- Listen to the response.
- Ask questions in a relaxed and casual manner.
- Let the interviewee talk; don't interrupt in the middle of an answer.
- Ask open-ended questions whenever possible.
- Ask follow-up questions when answers are unclear or eliciting additional information would be valuable.
- Encourage the interviewee to provide details and examples.
- Ask tough questions.
- Take notes on key ideas or opinions.

this interview to be a success? What information do I need to obtain? You might even want to pretend that you have already conducted the interview and ask yourself what you have learned from the questions you would have asked. Were your questions adequate at eliciting the information you hoped to obtain? If not, how could the interview have been structured differently?

Being aware of what needs to be accomplished will help you design questions to obtain the desired results. It will also help you explore unexpected issues that might arise.

Prepare the Questions

Occasionally, interviewers wing it. They prepare no questions in advance and instead make them up as they go along. This is an invitation to disaster. Few interviewers are capable of winging it. Research is conclusive on this. One researcher, for example, studied whether people who prepared for their interviews with candidates for a job were better at predicting these candidates' future job performance than people who did not prepare for the interviews. What the researcher found was that when the interviewers did not prepare questions in advance, their accuracy in predicting job performance was very poor. Accuracy was quite good, however, when the interviewers prepared their questions. Their predictions were even more accurate when the prepared questions were tailored to a specific job. The bottom line: Conducting a good interview requires preparation!

To prepare good questions, you must understand exactly what information you are trying to obtain. Once that has been decided, the next step is to design your questions so that they yield the information you want. Finally, you have to organize the questions in a logical sequence. Following the three steps we describe in the next sections will add considerably to the effectiveness of your interviews.

Design the Interview Thoughtfully

Interviews usually need to begin and end within a specific time frame. Most last for 30 to 60 minutes. Sometimes, interviews last longer than 60 minutes, occasionally they last several hours, but few are shorter than 30 minutes; you really cannot obtain much information in less time.

It is important to know how much time you have for the interview and to be sure you can ask all your questions in that time. This means that you will have to be very selective in what you ask and will have to cut some "good" questions. Some questions, though, are absolutely critical. Ensure that there is plenty of time to ask them.

Maintain Focus

Interviewees have a tendency to wander off the subject. They get caught up telling an interesting story, which may seem to go on forever. At other times, they may tell you specific information that isn't germane to the issue you're investigating. They may seem to be intentionally stalling, perhaps to avoid answering tough questions.

It is up to you to control the interview. There is only so much time, and there is usually a lot of information to gather. Make sure that the interviewee is sticking to the key questions. If the interviewee starts to stray, try to refocus attention on the topic at hand. This can be done by saying something like this: "That's a very interesting story; however, we are a little pressed for time and there are a couple of important issues I would like to get your opinion on."

Then ask the next question. Alternatively, you could say: "Could we hold that issue 'til the end? I want to make sure I have time to hear your

opinions on some other issues. Perhaps we can get back to this one later."
Then go on to the next question.

Stay Flexible

Although it is important to stay focused and stick with the questions during an interview, remaining flexible is also advisable. For example, not all
interviewees can supply the same amount of information about any particular issue or are willing to share that information. Thus, some people may
tell you a great deal in answer to a question, whereas others will have little
or nothing to say. You will want to spend more time on the questions that
are likely to yield the most valuable information and with the people who
are most forthcoming in supplying this information.

Flexibility is also useful in deciding when to end an interview and when
to extend it. There is nothing that says that an interview that is scheduled
for 1 hr has to run for exactly that long. If the interview isn't yielding much
information, end it early. If it is yielding a lot of information, allow extra
time if possible.

Don't get too rigid about the sequencing of questions, either. If an interviewee gives you information relevant to a different question from the one
you have just asked, consider focusing on that question and coming back
to the original question later. The sequence in which you ask questions is
not of paramount concern; it's better to obtain valuable information.

At other times, issues may arise that were not part of your agenda but
that are critical to the project at hand. For example, a consultant was interviewing personnel from a health care unit of a major hospital about the restructuring of their unit. During one of the interviews, one of the staff
members charged the chief medical officer with racism. The interviewer
decided to explore the charge in this and subsequent interviews as it appeared to be interfering with the success of the restructuring. This was a
judgment call on the part of the interviewer. You don't want to get involved in side issues unrelated to the focus of the interview; however, you
don't want to overlook discussing issues that might seem tangential
initially but that are actually extremely important.

Remain Unbiased

It is sometimes tempting to encourage an interviewee, albeit subtly, to answer a question a certain way or to let the client know you agree with the
interviewee on some issue. However, the purpose of an interview is to
gather unbiased information that accurately reflects the interviewee's be-
liefs. We cannot emphasize enough how important it is for the interviewer

to be aware of his or her biases and control any efforts to influence the respondent in that favored direction.

What do you think of the following questions, for example?

- Don't you think that the first advertisement gets the message across better than the second?
- Several people have said that the response time is much too slow. What do you think about the time it takes?

These are fairly obvious examples of questions in which the interviewee is trying to elicit certain answers. Bias can take many forms, however. Your tone of voice, for example, can convey the response you are looking for. Asking the same question in slightly different ways several times can have this effect as well. In this case, the interviewee may think he or she has given a "wrong" answer or a response other than the one the interviewer wanted. On the third time the interviewer asks the question, the interviewee is likely to give a different answer. If the interviewer records only the last answer, the data become biased and consequently inaccurately represent the interviewee's opinions.

Stay Politically Neutral

To be a good interviewer, one has to remain not only free of bias but also politically neutral. In other words, you must not try to gain favor with the interviewee by noting that you agree with some opinion he or she expressed; for example:

- I'm probably not supposed to say this, but I agree with your appraisal of the software package.
- You're very insightful about this issue. The more I hear, the more I'm siding with labor on this question.

Note that there is a difference between agreeing with a response and acknowledging a response. In the two preceding examples, the interviewer is definitely expressing agreement. However, the interviewer might say, "I see," or "I understand," or nod, any of which would indicate that the interviewer has heard the interviewee's response but neither agrees or disagrees with it.

Ask One Question

Good interviewers avoid asking several questions at once. When the interviewer asks multiple questions, the usual outcome is that the interviewee answers one question completely, one partially, and neglects to answer the others. Make sure you ask one question at a time, and give the interviewee plenty of time to answer.

Listen to the Response

This sounds simple, but it can be difficult to do: Listen to your interviewee's responses. Especially after doing many, many interviews, it can be tempting to daydream. Be assured, however, that if you're not present in the interview, your interviewee will detect your lack of interest. Consequently, the interviewee loses trust in the process and is less likely to reveal information that could be useful as you analyze a company's problem. Remaining attentive and interested in your interviewee helps build trusting relationships with your subjects and helps elicit more thorough and helpful responses. As Denny L. Brown, president of Linden Associates notes in the "From the Expert" section, being a good listener is not a passive sport! According to Brown, really listening to someone takes a lot of energy, but when you show interest in the person you are interviewing by being a good listener, he or she becomes more comfortable with you and the interview process, and you are more likely to get the needed information from your interviews.

Remain Relaxed and Casual

Interactions between you and the person you are interviewing should be relaxed and informal. Avoid cross-examination and the accusatory questioning style typical of attorneys in a courtroom. This is likely to lead to both defensiveness and resistance.

Let the Interviewee Talk

The purpose of an interview is to elicit information from someone, not to voice your own opinions. The person conducting the interview should talk only about 10% of the time; that is, the interviewee should be talking about 90%.

Giving your opinions on an issue steers interviewees to give the answers they think you are looking for and thus yields invalid information. This doesn't mean you should never give your opinion. During a discussion with a client about your contract, or a meeting in which the client wants to hear your approach to a problem, obviously you need to volunteer information. In interviews like these, you may be talking as much as 50% of the time.

From the Experts ...
Listen Up!
by Denny L. Brown, President, Linden Associates

In my roles both as controller of Owens Illinois and as an independent consultant, I've learned the importance of being a good listener when conducting an interview. A good listener puts an interviewee at ease, builds trust, and typically elicits much-needed information.

Whether you're discussing a consulting project with a prospective client, interviewing an assembly-line worker while doing research, or talking to a high-level executive about an ongoing project, good listening skills pay large dividends. Listening isn't a passive activity! If your objective is to collect information, it takes a lot of energy and intent listening. Over the years, the following tools have worked for me:

- Put the interviewee at ease. Don't launch immediately into the most important points you want to cover. A little small talk to crack the ice goes a long way. You'll elicit the best information if the person is relaxed and has considerable trust in you from the start.

- Do your homework. Have an interview plan and know which areas you want to pursue. Show interest in the interviewee and demonstrate value and appreciation for his or her opinions. Concentrate not only on what has been said but also what has not been said. Ask probing questions.

- Don't rush. Give the interviewee time to answer completely. Don't feel obligated to fill each momentary break with a new question—a little pause when no one is talking is not a bad thing.

- Be flexible in pursuing new topics that develop during the interview. Don't follow the agenda so rigidly that there's no chance to discuss a subject the interviewee initiates.

- Control the natural urge to talk. It's very difficult to be a good listener while talking or planning what you're going to say.

Again, being a good listener is not a passive activity. If you're conducting an interview, you need to expend considerable energy preparing it, properly conducting it, and going with the flow as ideas develop. It's like being the lineman whose role it is to make a hole for the running back who scores the touchdown. You, not me, can tell the 300-pound lineman that he has played a passive role! Similarly, it's not what *you* have to say that's important but what the interviewee has to say—most often, you have to actively "listen up" to get the message being sent.

Keep Questions Open Ended

Questions that can be answered with a simple "yes" or "no" or with a one-word answer do not yield much information and should be avoided as much as possible when you are interviewing someone. Such questions are designed to discourage interviewees from talking and may yield invalid information. "Have you stopped drinking excessively?" is an example of a yes-or-no question that puts the interviewee in a no-win and rather difficult position regardless of how he or she answers it. A better strategy is to ask questions that allow interviewees an opportunity to express and explain their opinions. Consider this question about a recent change in work rules: "Are you happy with the recent change in work rules?"

The question is very limiting in that it asks for a simple "yes" or "no" response and therefore gives respondents little or no opportunity to express their opinions about the change. A better question might be "How do you feel about the recent change in work rules?" Or perhaps "What do you think about the recent change in work rules?" These questions give the person being interviewed much more room to express his or her feelings and, consequently, yield considerably more information about the issue being discussed.

Try to begin questions with *what, when, how, why* or *where*. Questions that start this way are usually open ended.

Clarify

Open-ended questions give interviewees the chance to express their opinions. However, this doesn't mean that their responses are always clear or helpful. In fact, frequently they are general and vague and therefore subject to interpretation. For example, people often say things like there are "communications problems," "morale problems," the new manager is "too pushy," or that the return policy is "a disaster." What do these terms mean? Coming up with a good answer to that question is often not easy, particularly if you are interviewing someone you've never met.

When you are not clear what someone means, do not hesitate to follow up with another *what, why, how, when,* and *where* question. The following are some examples of questions designed to get an interviewee to explain a confusing response:

- What was said to give you the impression that ...
- What do you mean when you say that ...
- How could that have been handled to ... if ...
- Why did management reject the ...
- Where in the process do you think ...
- When did you realize that ...

Going back to the example we cited earlier, on the change of work rules, suppose that the interviewee had said that he or she had many problems with the change in work rules. To clarify, you might ask: "What do you mean when you say that you had many problems with the new work rules?" Or, better yet: "What kinds of problems are you having with the change in work rules?"

The interviewee might then respond "It has led to a lot of screw-ups," to which the interviewer might respond "How so? What kind of screw-ups are occurring?"

The interviewee might then respond "Well, we don't have any communication across shifts, so we don't know if the first shift had problems that we should know about."

The interviewer then asks "Can you give me a specific example of when a screw-up occurred across shifts that was related to the new work rules? What would be an example of that?"

The interviewee responds: "I think it was last Monday that the first shift had difficulty controlling the color on one of the Heidelberg presses, the number 6 press. They had to keep adjusting it to keep the color from blurring. We didn't know about it when we took over and made several runs before we discovered that the color was blurring."

The interviewer asks "How is that related to the new change in work rules?" and the interviewee responds "Under the old rules, we would have known about it because the first-shift operators would have briefed us. They would have explained the problem to us and told us how they were controlling it. Under the new rules, there is no briefing. They just stop and we start. Sometimes I don't even see them. I think the company is trying to save money with the new rules, but I think they will lose money in the long run."

As this example illustrates, it may take several probing questions to get to the level of detail so that the interviewer understands the problem or issue. The interviewer should not attempt to interpret the vague responses of interviewees and assume that the interpretation is correct. You have to get to a level of detail where there is no question as to what the interviewee is saying.

Ask for Detail and Examples

As noted earlier, it is important to get to a level of detail where there is full understanding of the problem. Developing an acceptable proposal, or a useful feedback report, or a set of recommendations, requires considerable understanding of the client's expectations, the work situation, or both. Often the only way to get this information is through interviews, and often you get only one shot at gathering it.

An additional advantage of asking interviewees for details and examples is that you often are expected to supply details and examples in your proposals and reports. Managers and employees routinely ask consultants for more details or ask them to give examples to support their conclusions. Being able to cite examples increases your credibility considerably.

Ask Tough Questions

In everyday conversation, most of us are pretty careful to avoid controversial, potentially embarrassing, emotional, or personal topics. We have learned over the years that to get along with others it is best to keep questions on a rather surface level unless the other person volunteers information that is more personal.

Unlike everyday conversation, interviews often focus on controversial topics. In fact, your credibility may depend on your ability to explore sensitive areas that are of concern to the interviewee but about which no one is willing to talk publicly.

If tough issues are not discussed and made public in reports and/or feedback sessions, interviewees will see your activities as evidence that nothing has changed, that the real problems are not getting discussed, and that it's business as usual. Word will quickly get around that you are not serious about dealing with the real issues and that your report to management is likely to say that everything is fine.

Don't avoid tough issues. Doing so could seriously jeopardize your credibility.

You also need to be alert to interviewees who hint at tough issues but don't raise them directly. For example, someone might give a fairly neutral answer to a question but add that "there are other problems" or "that's not the real problem" or "that's what management thinks." The interviewee is opening the door to talking about the real problem, and the interviewer should take the opportunity to probe further.

Take Notes

Taking notes is essential in any interview. Much too much important information is being communicated for you to trust your memory. What, then, are the most efficient ways to do this, and what should you record?

A common method is to put your (prepared) questions in an interview form, with enough space under each question to summarize each response. Use a separate form for each person you interview. Using this technique ensures that you cover all the key questions in the desired sequence and that each response gets recorded,

If you are conducting a large number of interviews, or there are several interviewers, using the same form for all the interviews will ensure that everyone is asked the same questions. In addition, using a form helps you organize the data if you are going to be summarizing the interviews in a report.

Now, what to record. You cannot possibly record everything mentioned during an interview and, it's not necessary. Record only the key words or phrases that relate to the questions being asked. (This is yet another reason it is so important to know the purpose of the interview before you write up your questions.)

There are two times during consulting assignments when taking good notes is especially important: (a) when interviewing prospective clients before writing proposals or contracts and (b) when conducting interviews for the purposes of gathering data and diagnosing problems. There is no need to record verbatim what was said in either of these situations; however, you should note key expectations and opinions.

We are frequently asked whether interviews should be tape recorded. There are only a few situations in which we recommend this. One problem is that interviewees may be reluctant to give honest responses if they are being recorded.

A more serious problem can occur when you begin to write the summary report. If the only record of what was said is on the tapes, you will probably have to listen to all of them (and take notes). This is extremely time consuming, particularly if you conducted many interviews. For this reason, tape recording makes sense only when you are concerned with quoting what one or more people said. For example, newspaper reporters frequently record interviews to ensure that interviewees are not misquoted. People writing books record interviews as well, so that they will be able to accurately summarize or quote something that was said a year or more later when they are writing the manuscript.

INTERVIEW FORMAT

Interviewers generally follow a format much like the one summarized in Table 5.2.

Beginning the Interview

Begin the interview by greeting the interviewee in a friendly manner. Introduce yourself, and show the interviewee to a seat. You will probably want to ask a question or two to establish rapport and help the interviewee feel comfortable. This strategy helps the person relax and makes the interview seem more like a friendly conversation than an interrogation.

There are a couple of approaches you can use to ensure that the atmosphere is fairly relaxed. One is to start with making small talk—that is,

TABLE 5.2
Standard Interview Format

- Greet the interviewee in a friendly manner and introduce yourself.
- Ask a question or two to establish rapport.
- Explain the purpose and length of the interview.
- Describe your expectations and assure confidentiality.
- Gather needed demographic information.
- Begin gathering general information about the topic, using open-ended questions.
- Move to more specific questions.
- Ask the interviewee to evaluate the problem/focus of the interview.
- Ask the interviewee for suggestions of ways to address the issue under discussion.
- Probe for clarity.
- Check to be certain you have covered all the important questions.
- Ask a final question that allows the interviewee to bring up any issues you may have overlooked.
- Thank the interviewee for his or her time and cooperation.

chatting about something that isn't work related. The weather, traffic, last night's ball game, or some significant local event or news story are among many possible topics.

Another approach is to talk informally about the company. For example, you might ask how long the interviewee has worked there, where he or she worked before, and how he or she came to work there. In contrast to starting with small talk, this approach sometimes yields information of value.

Whichever approach you use, make sure you maintain an informal and friendly demeanor. Try to appear relaxed and, as a signal that the initial conversation is off the record, don't take notes. You might also want to share some observations with the interviewee, being sure, of course, not to disclose information you're holding in confidence or that could bias the rest of the interview.

Explain the Purpose and Timeframe

It might be useful as you get down to the actual interview to remember the acronym *PAT*: *purpose, agenda,* and *time.* For example, you might want to say something like this:

> *John, as I noted on the phone, I wanted to go over some of the details of the project with you to make sure that I have the correct information before I put together the project proposal. I wanted to make sure that the proposal covered key objectives that you want to see accomplished. This should take about 30 minutes.*

For an interview on a new performance-appraisal process, you might want to start with something like the following:

> *As I indicated before, I'm Celeste Billings of the human resource department. I am part of a team studying the current performance-appraisal system here. We will be interviewing about 100 employees like you to get their impressions about the system as well as their suggestions of ways to improve it. I have a series of questions I'd like to ask you about the performance-appraisal system. It will take us about 45 minutes to complete the interview. I'd like you to answer as honestly as you can. I will be taking notes on what you tell me. Your responses, as well as those of the other employees, will be summarized in a report. The content of what you tell me will be summarized, but neither you nor any other employee will be identified by name.*
>
> *Before we start, do you have any questions about the study?*

In this introduction, Celeste very briefly introduces herself, describes the study, tells the interviewee the length of the interview, encourages honesty, and notes that the final report will not identify who said what. Finally, the interviewee is encouraged to ask questions. Encouraging a free exchange of questions is a good strategy; most interviewees probably won't know why you are interviewing them and may have concerns about the study or the interview. Answer all such questions directly and honestly.

Gathering Demographic Data

Next, many interviewers clarify what unit the interviewee works in, the unit's major responsibilities, how long the person has worked there, and the person's job duties. Information of this type is often helpful in interpreting interviewees' comments. You may find, for example, that the pattern of responses of a group of employees in one part of the company is different from the pattern of a group in another part.

Demographic questions are best asked directly. Thus, Celeste might say "Could you tell me what unit you are in and about your job duties?"

Another common technique is to begin by asking for general information about the topic of the interview. Celeste might ask "How does the performance-appraisal process work in your unit? What are the usual steps in the process?" Such questions are particularly helpful if practices vary across units. By asking this question, Celeste can get an idea not only about how the process works in the respondent's area but also about how this process differs from area to area within the company.

Moving Into the "Meat" of the Interview

Once you have established the purpose and time frame of the interview and asked the interviewee some demographic questions, it is time to get to the meat of the interview. It's best to start with very general, open-ended, questions. Celeste's might go something like this: "I'd like you to think for a moment about the current performance-appraisal process. How would you evaluate it? How effective has it been?" She might then ask a more specific question: "What are the parts of the process that you think are effective?" and then another specific question: "What are the parts that you think are not effective?"

After she has asked several specific questions, Celeste might ask the interviewee to evaluate the part of the performance evaluation that employees fill out (What parts does the interviewee consider useful? What parts are not useful? What does the interviewee think of the appraisal interview?)

Celeste would probably also like to hear the interviewees' suggestions about the new performance-appraisal system. Again, she might start with a general, open-ended question: "As we are redesigning a new performance-appraisal system, what are some of the things you think we should include?"

Once again, Celeste might want to ask about specific parts of the system, such as how the forms might be improved, how the interview might be more useful, and so on. Be sure to encourage the interviewee to offer details and examples.

Finishing Up

After you have finished asking all your questions, or just before you run out of time, you might want to briefly summarize the key points the interviewee has provided and ask whether you have accurately recorded his or her opinions. In addition to giving the interviewee a chance to correct any errors, summarizing in this way signals that you have made every effort to listen attentively and record the person's comments accurately.

Just before ending the interview, it's a good idea to ask a final question that encourages the interviewee to mention anything he or she might have forgotten or not had a chance to mention. You might say something like this: "Before we close this interview, I wonder if there is anything that you'd like to add, or any points we missed, that you would like to comment on," or perhaps: "Before we finish up, is there anything you'd like me to know about you or about the topic that we haven't talked about so far?" Be sure to give the interviewee time to think about your question as well as to answer it.

Finally, thank the person for his or her willingness to participate in your study and for his or her comments. You might want to add how the information collected from the interviews will be presented (in an oral presentation, written report, etc.) and/or the next step in the study.

CUSTOMIZING INTERVIEWS

The interview format we have just outlined may not apply in every situation. When interviewing prospective clients, for example, they are likely to want to know a lot about you, putting you more in the role of the interviewee than the interviewer. Such interviews involve a lot of sharing of information. By contrast, if you are conducting an interview designed to gather information about customers' opinions on a new product, or a new information system, you should probably say very little. As noted earlier, the most effective interviews are those in which the questions are prepared in advance and address the specific purpose of the interview. Thus, be sure you know the purpose of your interview and design the questions to meet that purpose.

SUMMARY

Interviews are used throughout a consulting project, from the initial conversation between the consultant and the prospective client to when a project is ending. As with other data collection techniques, collecting valid and reliable data is the key to conducting interviews that provide clients with valuable information. This chapter has described some of the basic techniques required for conducting effective interviews.

KEY SUCCESS FACTORS FOR CONDUCTING EFFECTIVE INTERVIEWS

- Prepare the questions and the agenda beforehand.
- Conduct the interview in a quiet, private setting free from distractions.
- Face the interviewee, make occasional eye contact, and acknowledge the interviewee's responses.
- Ask open-ended questions and probe to clarify and to encourage the interviewee to provide details and examples.
- Ask one question at a time, in a relaxed and casual manner.

- Keep the interview focused on the topic.
- Let the interviewee do the majority of the talking. In most interviews, the person you are interviewing should talk about 90% of the time.
- Ask tough questions.
- Take notes on key ideas or themes.

6

Preparing the Feedback/Assessment Report: Moving the Client to Action

Completing the data collection phase is a major accomplishment in a consulting project, but, as any researcher knows, data have little value unless they are analyzed and summarized in a manner that is useful to the reader. This is especially true of data collected by a consultant, as the whole purpose of data collection is to provide the client with information that will support taking action. Thus, the data you collect must be not only valid and useful but also presented so that the client can understand their implications.

The end of the data collection phase signals the beginning of the feedback phase, or, as it is increasingly called, the *assessment* or *analysis* phase of a project. During the assessment phase, you will analyze the findings of the research you conducted for the client and, as the term suggests, "feed back" or present these data to the client for review and assessment. Whether the document you present is called a *feedback report* or an *assessment report* has little or no bearing on its contents or format. However, you and the client should be in agreement on the terminology.

Depending on the nature of the study, a feedback report can directly influence organizationwide policy, staffing and layoffs, outsourcing, production, or a host of other matters. For the report to be effective—one that will be referred to in making decisions and that will help the client take appropriate action—you need to devote serious time and attention to preparing this document. Otherwise, as too often happens, the client will skim through the report and file it away, never to look at it again.

In this chapter we discuss how to prepare assessment reports that clients will appreciate receiving and that they will find helpful in making decisions concerning action to take on a project or in response to a study you and the client have been conducting. We recommend that assessment reports be fairly brief (fewer than 10 pages), that they cover three to seven major topics, and that the findings be presented both orally and in writing. Most important, if followed carefully, the report format discussed herein will ensure that the information is useful to the client and that the report is well organized and focused.

MEETING CLIENTS' EXPECTATIONS

Feedback reports come in all sizes and formats. They range from brief one-page summaries of major findings to documents of several hundred pages that include tables, figures, and statistical analyses. And, every once in a while, a client does not want a written report but merely wants to hear a presentation of the consultant's conclusions.

Some reports contain only data and analyses, some include the consultant's recommendation for actions to be taken, and some include recommendations plus a proposal from the consultant as to how she or he would implement the suggested actions.

The type of report to prepare is a function of your contract with the client. The report is one of the "deliverables" identified in your initial contract, and its form and content should be agreed on during these discussions. Regardless of what your contract says, however, always check with the client just before writing the report to make sure he or she still agrees with the format you will be using. You might also want to discuss whether the client wants both a written report and oral presentation. Now, as during other phases of the project, managing the client's expectations is paramount. Checking periodically to ensure that you and the client are on the same page is a good way to eliminate misunderstandings and surprises.

This chapter does not cover all report formats but instead focuses on the most common way consultants present their findings—that is, in a fairly brief written report, covering three to seven major topics. In chapter 7 we discuss the basics of making oral presentations based on this report.

WHAT CONSTITUTES A GOOD REPORT?

To be considered good, or effective, a report must meet four criteria. The report must:

1. Provide information that is practical and useful to the client.
2. Be easy for the client and other managers to read and understand.
3. Be concise.

4. Support conclusions, recommendations, and plans of action with solid data.

We now discuss each of these points one at a time.

Practical and Useful

Clients hire consultants for help in addressing issues that they are often burning to answer: whether to reorganize a department; revamp a policy; or, as we discussed in chapter 3, change the way a process, such as distribution, is handled. First and foremost, a feedback report needs to focus on the issue the client has said needs to be addressed. In other words, there needs to be a clear and direct link between the data, analysis, summary statements, and recommended actions and the issue the client has identified as requiring attention.

Ideally, the report should focus on a limited number of points that are central to the concerns of the client. Too much data or too many recommendations are overwhelming. It is better to identify a limited number of major issues.

Easy to Read and Easy to Understand

To be useful, the report needs to speak the language of the managers who are responsible for making decisions related to the issue the report addresses. Writing a report is not the same as writing a paper for a course in a university. A report for a client is not the place to show off knowledge of business theory or to muse about philosophy. It should be written in the client's language and should be free of professional jargon.

Concise

The typical feedback report is between 2 and 10 pages in length. Clients do not have the time or the patience to wade through reams of paper, particularly if the findings are also being presented at a meeting. Clients want reports that are concise and to the point.

There are exceptions to this guideline. If a report is going to be considerably more detailed and therefore longer than the average 2 to 10 pages, this should be decided when you and the client negotiate the contract. Both of you need to understand the parameters of the project. For example, a major medical center contracted with a consulting firm to do a 1-year in-depth analysis of its operations and market opportunities and to compare the results with those of other medical centers. The resulting document consisted of two large volumes plus a 30-page executive summary. In this case, given the scope of the study and the level of detail required, no one was surprised by the size of the document.

Supported by Solid Data

One of the reasons clients hire consultants is that they need data to support their taking or not taking action. Thus, feedback reports should be based on facts, not personal opinions. The client will want to know how you arrived at your findings and conclusions. Thus, it is critical that any conclusions be well founded. Whenever possible, support your findings with hard data (means, standard deviations, and ranges). For example, "Ninety percent of the employees think the equipment is outdated and negatively affects their productivity" is a much more powerful, fact-based statement than saying that "Many employees think the equipment is outdated and negatively affects their productivity."

Consultants are often hired to address controversial issues. Be prepared for someone to challenge your conclusions. When your findings are based on solid data, however, it is much more difficult to dispute the validity of your conclusions. Solid data are your best defense when questions arise about your findings.

Although it is important to base your report on solid data, Malou Roth, founder of People First, a consulting company, shows in the "From the Experts" section for this chapter how too much data can sometimes paralyze the data reporting process. Roth notes how too much data can be as much a problem as too little data and says that finding the right balance is a key to successful report writing. She writes about the difficulty of managing the client who wants to continue to collect data instead of organizing the data in a meaningful way that allows one to make recommended changes.

OVERVIEW

Suppose for a minute that you have conducted 1-hr interviews with 30 employees, including managers, in your client's organization. In addition, your coworker has spent 12 days reviewing company documents and records. This effort has generated a large volume of data. Summarizing the findings sounds like a daunting task, but by following a few rules, it actually will be fairly easy.

Find Major Themes

Your task is to separate the "vital few"—themes—from the "trivial many" that have no direct impact on the question under consideration. Usually

From the Experts …
Is There Such a Thing as Too Much Input to Report?
by Malou Roth, President, People First

I was once hired by a small but up-and-coming high-tech firm with an unusually well-staffed human resources/organizational development (HR/OD) department. The firm wanted me to conduct some management and employee training. The stated objective was to improve the skills of managers to manage their people and to help employees strengthen their skills so as to help improve efficiency and productivity overall. Previously, the company had offered very little training in these areas. The director of OD and the vice president of HR decided that they did not want "off-the-shelf" material yet resisted the idea of interviewing a cross-section of managers and employees to assess their needs. When I tried to discuss these decisions, they viewed my comments as disagreement, not as an attempt to help them discover how to provide some customized training. Instead of talking to managers and employees to determine what training was needed, they had done a number of online surveys using generic software they had moderately adapted. The survey feedback was all over the place, with managers and employees asking for a huge range of training that would have been nearly impossible to do. There didn't seem to be any consensus on what was a priority. These results launched more surveys to try to identify more specifically what people wanted, and, of course, this generated more results.

Why all these surveys? And how was I to interpret all the data and eventually write a report that would help them determine what training programs to design and teach? It turned out that, the year before, the director of OD had purchased and installed a fairly expensive online learning system containing a wide variety of training programs. After analyzing one of the early surveys, the director was very dismayed to learn that employees did not like the online solution. They wanted classroom training with a facilitator/instructor, colleagues, and donuts.

In an effort to avoid another misstep, the director of OD and the vice president of HR were being overly cautious about how to determine what training to offer. The repeated surveys gleaned more information than they needed and prompted them to become virtually paralyzed about how to proceed. They seemed unable to decide where to start and resisted my suggestions to select some of the frequently heard needs from the survey results and just get started. Writing a report from the myriad of data was virtually impossible. The director sometimes seemed like a kid in a candy store; he had generated so much information, he couldn't figure out what to select, and he seemed overly anxious about making a mistake and choosing the wrong workshop to start the training, so he just kept asking for everything, making summary data reports nearly impossible to achieve.

I advised them to talk to some of the senior managers, from whom they needed support and money for any initiatives. I suggested they present an overview report of the survey results to show that employees and managers seemed open to a wide selection of topics for training. We would then ask the senior managers which competencies they felt were most in need of improvement. This process would make report writing and summary of the data much easier and many times more useful. In addition, it would allow them to share the decision making with the senior management and also get their support for the training. The moral of this story is that, in order to determine what the needs and priorities are and write a good report, you have to have start with a data collection method that collects just the right data and nothing more!

the vital few become obvious as you review the data. Employees may mention a concern or voice a complaint again and again in interviews or in responses on a questionnaire. Consultants frequently hear, for example, about the lack of integration of a company's computer system, equipment that frequently fails, bosses who don't communicate clearly, and product lines that have had dramatic downturns in sales. When there are consistent patterns of responses over many interviews or questionnaires, they become vital instead of trivial findings.

The feedback report should focus on a few—probably no more than seven—issues. Taking action to address a few major concerns will move the organization ahead considerably faster and more easily than spending a lot of time dealing with numerous minor complaints.

Identify Relevant Issues

The issues or ideas outlined in the report should provide the answers, or guidelines for answering, the problem or executing the project the client has said needs addressing. You may uncover a variety of interesting issues and problems while collecting the data. However, the report should focus only on those issues that directly affect the concerns mentioned in your contract. Issues that do not influence the topic at hand can be handled in another document.

Focus on "Action" Issues

Given the opportunity to vent their concerns and frustrations about their work lives, interview subjects often talk about matters that are far removed from the issue the client needs addressing. Issues such as the economy or outsourcing may be of major concern to employees but of little or no relevance to the issue under consideration with the client. What's more, the client may not be able to do much or anything about the problem unrelated to the project. The client can change the performance management system, or implement better quality control, or add a second shift. However, the client cannot change the national economy and, more important, the client did not hire you to address individuals' personal problems.

Emphasize Issues That Can Be Handled Quickly

Clients want to see results. They, their staff, and their superiors are likely to be willing to devote more energy and commitment to projects that will produce quick, visible outcomes. Results are energizing. Projects that go on forever without producing positive outcomes are doomed to die.

Focus on Issues That People Agree Need Attention

People are rarely motivated to work on projects about which they are not excited, or to solve problems or revamp processes they don't think merit attention. If there is little energy to work on an issue, regardless of how important you perceive it to be, not much is likely to happen. It is always best to concentrate on issues that people are concerned about and agree need serious attention (as shown by your data).

SUMMARIZING THE DATA

Let's go back to the example used earlier. You have interviewed 20 people for 1 hr each, which obviously could produce a lot of information. How do you convert this volume of data into a concise and usable summary?

The first step is to begin identifying the major themes or issues. To begin, go through the notes you took during the interviews (and/or the notes other people took), one at a time, and record the major issues that were mentioned. Some people keep a tally, using separate sheets of paper for each issue. By the time you have finished reviewing the final interview, you will have a list of the major issues, the number of people who raised each issue, and notes on each person's comments. Using these notes, you can easily write a report summarizing the major issues that need addressing, supported by anonymous quotes from the data.

Some software programs allow data to be sorted on the basis of keywords. If the interviews were transcribed so they can be read on a computer, you will be able to do a quick sort of the data based on keywords/issues. As with the system described earlier, the comments so generated can then serve as a basic outline for the report.

Writing the report is even easier if you conducted surveys, such as employee or customer satisfaction questionnaires. If respondents answered a multiple-choice survey, for example, a computer-generated scoring program can do much of the work of summarizing the data. Depending on the sophistication of your computer skills (and the time you or your staff have to do this), you may also enter the data and analyze it yourself. In addition to overall scores, you probably will want to analyze mean scores for each question as well as by unit, customer group, or other segments (e.g., functional area, gender, age, department, etc.). You may also want to analyze the range of responses and standard deviations for individual questions, which tells you how much dispersion (difference) there is among respondents. If the standard deviation is large, there was what is known as *heterogeneity* in respondents' answers—that is, not a lot of agreement. If the standard deviation is small, then agreement was more widespread. Standard deviations can indicate widespread support for a change in an organization.

Some scoring programs can convert raw data directly into a narrative format. These are especially popular among consultants who specialize in survey research.

Assuming that you are analyzing the data yourself, instead of relying on a computer program, the first step in analyzing survey data is to identify which items generated the highest scores and which generated the lowest. For example, a survey conducted for a restaurant might indicate that customers were very satisfied with the quality of the food but very dissatisfied with the length of time it takes to get served. In this case, the feedback report would focus on both the areas that the restaurant is handling well—namely, food quality—and those that need improvement—the time required to provide service. More detailed analysis, such as the mean scores for each question, or even for each customer, could be included in an appendix.

We recommend following a similar procedure to summarize data generated from organization records. For example, a consultant who was hired to look at "significant problems" in a manufacturing facility found, after examining company records, that a high percentage of the company's products were rejected at final inspection, that there were no company-wide selection criteria used to choose new hires, that neither new hires nor supervisors received any training, and that the annual rate of turnover among line personnel was a dismal 65%. These issues appeared to be interrelated and to have a direct impact on the significant problems of concern to the client. The consultant documented these problems in a report and assisted the manufacturing group in discovering the causes of the problems and developing corrective actions.

In another case, a medical supply company hired a marketing consultant to study its declining sales. The consultant began the analysis by examining the company's sales records, particularly sales by market segment. Much to everyone's surprise, the data revealed that sales to small hospitals had been increasing—at about 15% each year. However, sales to large facilities had been dropping—at an annual rate of about 5%. The consultant's report documented the sales trends by market segment and, in the next phase of the project, helped management design another study, this time to focus on the causes of the decline in the large-systems market.

In all of the examples just cited, the consultant analyzed and summarized the data and identified a few major issues that, if resolved, would move the company forward. These are also good examples of how consultants can contribute to the success of their clients' companies.

CONTENT OF A REPORT

The common denominator among written reports is that they all include a data summary and analysis. As we mentioned at the beginning of this chapter, where they differ is in whether they contain recommendations and, if they do, whether they also include a plan for implementation.

Reports Containing Data Summaries Only

It is not uncommon for a consultant to be hired simply to conduct a study and write up the results. For example, consultants are frequently hired to administer employee job satisfaction surveys, in which case the deliverable may be simply a short report on the survey results, broken down by plant location and work unit. The hiring organization may well have extensive resources and capabilities and prefer to do the rest of the work from within, including analyzing the results, preparing a plan of action, and implementing changes.

For strategic reasons, some consultants prefer not to provide recommendations. Included in this group are consultants who subscribe to the *action research model*. A basic assumption of this model is that if clients are involved in analyzing data and determining actions to be taken, they will be more committed to carrying out those actions than if the consultant merely presents them with recommendations and action plans. Regardless of the reason that the client and consultant have contracted for a relatively bare-bones report, the assumption is that the client will assume responsibility for taking any and all action once the data have been collected.

Reports Containing Recommendations

Reports containing recommendations are far more common than those that do not contain them. Most clients view consultants as experts in particular areas and expect any consultant they hire to recommend actions based on this expertise. After all, they would argue, isn't that what consultants are supposed to do? Why hire one if you're not getting expert advice about what actions to take? Moreover, the client is never under any obligation to accept or to implement the consultant's recommendations, and many organizations do not.

One of the reasons for hiring a consultant is that they provide an objective, unbiased, and expert perspective on a problem. With this recommendations-included format, you offer such a perspective.

Reports Containing Implementation Plans

Many major consulting firms routinely prepare reports that contain not only data summaries and recommendations for action but also a proposal on how the consultant or consultant's firm would implement the recommendations. These proposals usually include specific action steps, time-lines, and the costs to implement the action.

Consultants are generally keen to prepare implementation plans for clients. For most large projects, the real money is in the implementing phase, not in conducting the research and doing assessments. In fact, some firms will do brief assessments for no charge in the hope that the firm will be awarded the contract for implementation. There are certain advantages to preparing this type of report; in particular, providing an implementation plan enables a project to move quickly from the assessment phase to action. If the client agrees with the analysis and recommendations, going ahead and taking action is then usually relatively easy. When clients ask for an implementation plan or a proposal, it usually means they are serious about acting on the consultant's findings.

Deciding What to Include

Which of the three report formats to use should depend on what the client wants or expects you to include in the report, which is often discussed in the context of the contract, and what will best serve the client's interests. If the client has no expertise in the area in question, it is often a good idea to suggest that you include recommendations, and perhaps a plan for implementing them.

In any case, you and the client need to reach an agreement on what to include in the report during the contract phase of the project. This will avoid any misunderstanding. For example, if the client expects recommendations but you don't include them, the client is likely to think that you did not deliver on what you promised. Likewise, if the client asks you to add sections to the report that you didn't expect to write, you are likely to feel that you have had to devote more time and attention to the report than you budgeted.

REPORT FORMATS

Although the format of the report will vary depending on your purpose, audience, and style, a widely used format has evolved. This is the structure we discuss here. You should feel free to adapt this structure to meet your project needs.

Cover Page

Feedback reports usually contain a cover page giving the title, the author, and the date. (See Appendix for an example.) Alternatively, the first page of text may be in memorandum format and give the name of the person to whom the report is directed (the client), who the report is from (the consultant), the date, and the subject.

Executive Summary

Every report should begin with an executive summary that highlights in bullet points the main findings of the study. Unfortunately, many clients never read past this page. Thus, you should treat this as a very important part of the report.

Purpose of Study

Many people who read your report won't remember why you conducted the study or why you were hired; others may never have heard of the study. This is the place to state the reason the study was undertaken. You should also include a statement about the benefits the client can expect from addressing the issue.

Method

Although a feedback report is not like a research article published in an academic journal, it still needs to include a brief description of how the study was conducted. For example, if the consultant conducted interviews, it is important to note the following: how long they lasted (number of minutes or hours), whether they were face-to-face interviews or done by telephone, how many people were in the sample, who was interviewed (categories of people, not names), how they were selected, the dates of the interviews, and a brief summary of the questions that were asked. In addition to these details, you should thank interviewees and company officials for their cooperation and willingness to share information.

Treatment of Data

This section provides a roadmap to the rest of the report. For example, are all the data presented, or just the major results? If the latter, on what basis were these results selected? How will the data be reported (e.g., means, standard deviations, ranges)?

Presentation of Results

This is the meat of the report. Most consultants use one of four formats to organize and present their results.

Format 1.   Focus only on the problems you uncovered, with data to back them up. This format may be used to address specific issues, such as what is wrong with a company's system for quality control. Thus, the report would outline the six problems the consultant thinks are wrong with the process for quality control.

Format 2.   Present positive findings first, followed by a section on areas needing improvement. This format is especially useful when a fair amount of the findings reflect badly on a unit within the company. In particular, the consultant may be concerned about demoralizing the client and about giving the impression that nothing positive is occurring in the unit under study. Most units have elements that work well. Starting the results section by commenting on these elements may make it easier for management to take corrective action on the area needing improvement. This format is also useful for summarizing information obtained through an audit of a department or division, as opposed to a study of a few specific issues.

Format 3.   Frame the discussion of findings around issues/questions the client has identified as needing to be addressed. This format is especially effective if the client wants specific questions answered. In a marketing study, for example, the client may want to learn about its competition. Findings may shed light on such specific issues as the advantages of competitors' products, how the client's products compare with those of its competitors, and so forth. In this case, the data would be organized around these key questions.

Format 4.   Devise a list of categories relevant to the project (e.g., leadership, communication, interpersonal relationships, rewards) and summarize findings accordingly. This format is used most often when the client or consultant is looking at the various pieces that make up a system, as in a management or quality audit. For example, the consultant might audit the organization using the criteria to evaluate companies being considered for the National Quality (Baldrige) Award. For each item, the consultant would discuss the scores for the unit being studied.

If the client has asked you to recommend an action plan, these recommendations should go in the next section. If you are not providing recommendations, then this is the final section of the assessment.

Recommendations

As discussed earlier, some reports contain a recommended plan of action, and some do not. The types of recommendations consultants make are practically limitless, from advising organizations to start a quality-improvement program to suggesting the company hire three more people in sales or marketing. Regardless of the recommendations, they should be as specific as possible and as closely as possible address the problem or issue the client has asked you to address.

You may also want to include a plan for implementing the recommendations. For example, if a company were having a problem with high turnover among middle managers, you might suggest that you could help design and facilitate a 3-day retreat for the company's senior-level executives to devise a strategy to address this problem. In addition, you might propose that you assist in the design of a follow-up program, to ensure that action is taken after the retreat is over. Included in the report would be a tentative timetable, a budget, and a summary of the benefits to be expected from these actions.

Summary

Lengthy reports often end with a summary, in which the consultant reviews the major findings of the study.

Many consulting firms bind their reports. The firm's logo is often on the cover, as well as on the first and last pages. Examples of complete reports are presented at the end of this chapter (see Appendix).

HANDLING PRICKLY SITUATIONS

On occasion, difficult situations arise during the data collection phase of a project. You should definitely give serious thought to whether to discuss these situations in the feedback report.

Controversial Issues

Deciding how much to include in the report about a controversial situation, such as a conflict between subordinates and their superiors or between groups of employees, is not always easy. As a general rule of thumb, controversial issues and situations should be discussed only if they relate directly to the primary problem or issue at hand. In fact, you may have been brought in, at least in part, because you could provide a fresh perspective on this difficult situation. Avoiding touchy issues altogether will seriously undermine your credibility.

Irrelevant But Critical Issues

At some time, you are likely to learn about an issue that may be of major consequence to the organization but irrelevant to your inquiry. If the overall issue is important, you should inform the appropriate persons via memo or by e-mail. Such information should not generally be included in the report.

Naming Names

During interviews, respondents often refer to individuals by name: "John always sends the requests to Purchasing, which causes another delay" or "Joan's group has a lot of problems keeping up with the requests." Most reports focus on system-level analysis—that is, on such matters as how to improve the system for processing new orders or for distributing product—not on specific individuals. In other words, the focus of the report should generally be on the structure or flow of a system, not on people. The obvious exception is when the actions of specific people or groups are the subject of the study or have a major impact on the issue at hand. In this case, naming names is not only appropriate but also necessary.

Name-Calling, Gossip, and Accusations

Much as naming names often diverts attention from the real problems at hand, repeating gossip or accusing individuals of wrongdoing deflects attention from the issues that need to be addressed. Such behavior does not contribute to clarifying issues or solving problems, instead, it usually interferes with their resolution. In some cases, however, you may be able to gain insight into a problem by analyzing how, and why, gossiping or similar behavior is occurring.

In this chapter we have outlined a step-by-step process to help both the novice and seasoned consultant prepare feedback/assessment reports that help move clients to action. In chapter 7 we discuss how the information in a feedback/assessment report can be presented at a meeting.

KEY SUCCESS FACTORS FOR WRITING EFFECTIVE ASSESSMENT REPORTS

- Before writing the report, check with the client to determine the appropriate format, as well as how the report should be presented.

- Keep feedback reports brief—fewer than 10 pages—and focus only on the 3 to 7 issues of most concern to the client.
- Begin with an executive summary—remember, many clients will read nothing else!
- Support conclusions and recommendations with solid data.
- Strive to make the report easy to read and to understand. Avoid professional or consultant jargon.
- Emphasize actions that can be implemented quickly and easily.
- Focus on system wide issues, never on pointing fingers at individuals.

Appendix

Sample Feedback Report

To: Board of Directors and Staff Central Region Service Center
Date: July 8, 2006
From: Brayden Gregory, Founder, Do The Right Thing Consulting Co.
Subject: SUMMARY OF INTERVIEW DATA

Executive Summary: Based on Interviews on the Operations of the Service Center

Service Center has notable strengths, including employee pride, a respected staff, a cooperative workforce, and excellent facilities.

Areas Needing Improvement

- Direction of center
- Decision making
- Communications
- Hiring process
- Compensation system
- Performance-appraisal system

Recommendations

- Develop a strategic planning process.
- Revitalize management council.
- Publish a monthly newsletter and have all-staff meetings every 3 months.
- Develop a hiring manual.
- Review job classifications.
- Develop guidelines for procedures for annual performance assessments.

Purpose of the Study

Over the past 2 years, the Central Region Service Center has experienced a series of changes, including expansion of its staff and service and reorganization of the service-delivery system. Now that the reorganization has been completed, the Board of Directors thought it was an opportune time to review the operations of the center, with particular reference to the general impression of the staff concerning the recent reorganization, and to identify any issues that have been left unresolved.

With that goal in mind, the Board of Directors contracted the services of Do the Right Thing to interview the staff of the center and to report the findings on these interviews to the board and to the staff of the center. The report would then be used as a basis for instituting action designed at correcting any outstanding issues.

Method

All full-time and part-time employees of the Central Region Service Center were interviewed individually (50 interviews). Although many questions were open-ended, we primarily conducted structured interviews, which enabled us to better compare and contrast responses. These interviews took place on May 5 and 6 at the administrative offices. Each interview was conducted face to face and lasted approximately 1 hr. Respondents were asked to respond to each question on a 1–5 scale, with 5 being *strongly agree* and 1 being *strongly disagree*.

In addition to the questions to which responses were to be given on a 1–5 scale, each employee was asked a series of open-ended questions, including "What things are working well on your job? What things are causing problems on the job? What do you need to be more effective? What is your evaluation of the recent reorganization? What issues or problems have remained unresolved since the reorganization?" The employees were asked for their honest opinions and were told that their names would not be used in the report. They were also told that all data summaries would be in aggregate form and that any quotes would not be attributed to individuals.

The executive director and the support staff were extremely cooperative in arranging the interviews. The staff, with few exceptions, was very open and helpful in sharing their observations with the interviewers.

Treatment of the Interview Data

Data obtained from the interviews were grouped and summarized on the basis of respondents' comments on the reported strengths of the center and the areas they thought needed improvement. Patterns in responses were noted, based on means, standards, and ranges for each question. Given the small sample size, we did not use standard deviations (general similarities or differences in responses).

The purpose of the study was to review the general operations of the center. Therefore, we have summarized only those strengths or problems that several staff members mentioned. We have not added our own comments, and, as the interviewees were promised, we do not identify anyone who was interviewed by name.

The reported strengths of the center are presented first, followed by the areas identified as needing improvement.

Strengths of the Center

The employees reported that the center had several notable strengths. Summarized below are the strengths mentioned in our interviews.

1. Eighty-five percent of the respondents noted that the center is a valuable asset to the central region and performs a valuable service to its clients. Ninety-three percent are proud to be identified with the center. Eighty-seven percent also think that the people of the central region, both clients and others, have a high respect for the service the center provides.

2. Workers respect the center's staff; 90% strongly agreed with this statement. Eighty-eight percent of the employees thought the staff was competent, well trained, and professional. Eighty-seven percent indicated that they would not hesitate to recommend that a client come to the center, because they thought the client would receive excellent service.

3. In general, the staff like working at the center. Eighty-nine percent reported that the center is a good place to work. Some specific comments were that they were proud to work at the center, staff members were allowed the freedom to practice their profession, there is a minimum of bureaucratic interference with the delivery of services, that one's ability and skills are respected, and that there is a professional climate at the center.

4. There is good cooperation among the professional staff, among the support staff, and between the support staff and professional staff (85%, 86%, and 88% responded *agree* or *strongly agree*, respectively). There were many comments to the effect that "we work as a team here," "people are really supportive of each other," and "you always can turn to someone here for help if you have a problem."

5. Ninety-one percent think the physical facilities are ample and allow staff to perform their jobs effectively. The staff is overwhelmingly pleased (90% agree) with the new administrative offices.

6. Staff view the growth of the center quite positively, since the center now provides many more services for the residents of the central region (88% agree). The staff was very complimentary of the leadership of the center for advocating and obtaining the increased services (86% agree).

7. The staff made generally positive comments about the recent restructuring of the center (88%). Although it was disruptive to certain units, and there was often inadequate communication about the changes, the staff generally thinks the restructuring was necessary because of the center's increased service responsibilities. The staff perceives the new structure as accomplishing what it was designed to do—that is, enable the center to deliver basic services more effectively (90% agree).

Areas Needing Improvement

Below is a summary of the issues the staff mentioned as needing improvement. The issues listed here were raised in one form or another by staff members, and among these respondents, the levels of dissatisfaction were consistently high. These areas clearly warrant further attention. The next step is to explore these problems further and, subsequently, to devise actions to correct these difficulties.

1. There was some confusion about the direction the center is taking. What services are going to be expanded? What services are going to be added? What services will be discontinued? Eighty-four percent of the staff noted the need for a strategic plan for the center so that staff can better understand the new direction the center is headed and everyone will know what is expected of them. One hundred percent of the respondents making this recommendation thought that the entire staff should have input into the plan as a way to heighten awareness of it and commitment.

2. Eighty-six percent of the employees felt that the general staff at the center have been losing decision-making power over the last year or so. Eighty-five percent noted that there was less "shared decision making" than before the reorganization. Ninety percent said that it is not clear who is making policy decisions and whether any staff input is elicited before making decisions.

Related to the above point, 85% of the staff noted that the Management Council has had less of a role in the overall operations of the Center over the last year. In unstructured interviews, many staff members

(50%) noted that the Management Council had seemed to work well in the past as a means for providing input from each of the programs as well as for communicating information to staff in the various programs.

3. Eighty-five percent of the staff suggested that better mechanisms of communication should be developed so that the staff can be kept current on changes in policies and responsibilities. In the unstructured interviews, several people ($n = 25$) cited the shifting of intake responsibilities that occurred in January, which was not announced to the general staff, causing considerable confusion.

Data from the unstructured interviews indicate a failure to communicate to other programs about decisions, even when these decisions impact the other programs (30 people with unprompted comments). Each program seems to be focused inward, and sometimes people do not realize that changes in their program may affect others.

4. Ninety-two percent of the respondents reported that there has not been any consistency lately in the staff's involvement and input into hiring. Sometimes staff are involved, and sometimes they are not. These 92% of the respondents thought that having staff involved in the hiring of employees would lead to better hiring decisions.

5. There was general and serious concern about compensation (89% of respondents). Most employees (89%) felt that, in general, the pay at the center was "fairly competitive" with that in other agencies. However, several employees (32%) noted, "Pay is a mystery around here." Although salaries are not public, there is a general perception that there are inconsistencies in salaries and fringe benefits. For example, it is generally believed that all of the seven program directors are paid according to a different pay scale even though they have approximately the same workload and duties (40 volunteered this comment in an interview). Likewise, there is the perception that there are other salary discrepancies (35 comments in this regard).

Some staff expressed concern that employees do not understand how salaries and raises are determined, there are inconsistencies in pay for similar jobs, no recognition for length of service or experience, no increase in pay for increases in job responsibilities, and no links between pay and performance. Some felt that salaries and raises are arbitrary and that some employees are underpaid.

6. Sixty-five percent of the employees noted that they understood that every employee was supposed to have an annual performance appraisal. However, this policy is not being applied consistently across units. Some staff have annual appraisals, while others claim not to have had one in 3 years. A related concern was what the appraisal is used for. Is it the basis for annual raises? If so, what happens if someone hasn't received an appraisal?

(The feedback report could end at this point. You would present the findings and then help the client explore these issues further, as well as assist the client in deciding what actions to take to correct the problems. Alternatively, you could make recommendations about how to correct the problems and focus the discussion in the feedback meeting on whether to accept the recommendations and, if so, how to implement them. If the client expects you to make recommendations, the report might continue as follows.)

Recommendations

As noted above, the staff has generally positive feelings about the center and its leadership and is pleased with the center's services and contribution to the community. Most view the recent reorganization positively and consider it a success. The interviews also uncovered several issues of concern, however, many of which are issues that were not resolved during the reorganization. Although these issues are not of the magnitude as to be detrimental to the center in the short term, they need to be addressed as soon as possible. To address these concerns, the following actions are recommended. They are recommended in the order in which they are discussed above.

1. *Develop a 5-year strategic plan.* It is further recommended that all center staff be involved in developing this plan. One model that has been demonstrated to be effective is to hold a 2-day off-site retreat in which the directors and all staff participate. This would generate the key information for the plan. On the basis of this information, a committee would then draft the plan, which would be presented to the entire group for revision and approval. This approach would create the sense of there being a common direction fairly quickly. It would also maximize staff input and commitment to the plan's goals and strategies.

2. *Revitalize the Management Council and give it the authority to take an active role in decision making that affects the center.* The managers on the council would be expected to seek input from their direct reports and to keep them informed about the council's deliberations and decisions.

3. *Make an effort to increase communication.* If a decision affects all the staff, then memos should be sent to all employees. In addition, a monthly newsletter should be sent to all staff and interested parties that includes, among other information, news about changes in any of the programs. Finally, all-staff meetings should be held every 3 months to update the staff on changes and, more important, to provide a mechanism for answering staff questions.

4. *The Management Council should develop a manual on the policies and procedures for hiring staff.* Included should be a process to ensure staff involvement and input.

5. *A review should be conducted of the job classifications and salaries for all job positions in the center.* The goal of this review would be to establish a classification and compensation system that equates salary fairly with responsibility and that provides a basis for the job classification and compensation system that will be used throughout the center.

6. *The Management Council should establish guidelines and procedures for annual performance appraisals.* It is essential that these procedures be applied consistently throughout the center. Among the issues to be decided is whether there should be a merit pay system. In either event, appropriate forms need to be developed.

(The report could end here. However, if you wish to be involved in implementing the recommendations, then a brief description of how you propose to help, as well as your fee for providing that service, could follow each of the recommendations. Alternatively, this information could be in a separate section following the recommendations. In either case, you and the client will need to sign a new contract to implement the recommendations.)

7

Presenting the Findings: Moving From Diagnosis to Commitment to Action

Some consultants think that once the feedback report is completed, they have completed their work—that is, that the report contains the full spectrum of their insights and wisdom. The reality is that a feedback report has no value unless the client understands the implications of the findings *and* takes action based on the consultant's research.

We believe that although feedback reports are very important, the consultant's job certainly should not stop there. The consultant has an obligation to ensure that the client not only understands what data were collected, what analyses were performed, and how these address the question the client wants answered but also whether and, equally important, what additional data or analyses are needed to address the client's questions or problems. Among just a few of the issues the client might want to address further are the trends the data reveal concerning the organization's financial status or how to reverse high employee turnover. The client may also ask the consultant to recommend actions the client organization should take in response to the study's findings. Finally, the client may want the consultant to examine issues such as the costs and long-term effects of taking these actions.

An effective consultant is one who not only summarizes findings but also assists clients in taking action. A report that sits on a shelf or in someone's file cabinet is totally useless. In contrast, a report that prompts action adds value to the organization and is a cornerstone to building a better run, more efficient organization.

One of the distinguishing characteristics between consultants whose reports sit in file cabinets and those who lead clients to implement changes (and hire these consultants for the implementation stage of a project) is how these consultants deliver their research findings. Some simply mail in their reports to the client along with their bill—and, not surprisingly, many of these reports end up in file drawers gathering dust. A far more effective approach is to present the findings in a face-to-face presentation, either for just your contact at the organization or for others there as well. Larry Anders, from Anders & Associates, and Sherry Camden-Anders, from Alliant International University, discuss in the "From the Experts ..." section for this chapter the importance of orally presenting study findings. For Camden and Camden-Anders, an oral presentation of study findings creates a collaborative environment that encourages a commitment to action. They claim that oral presentations provide yet another opportunity to get the client on board with implementing any recommended changes. In this chapter we discuss many of the issues to be considered in making such presentations.

From the Experts ...
Presenting the Findings
by Larry Anders, Anders & Associates, and Sherry Camden-Anders,
Alliant International University

As organization development (OD) consultants, we generally contract to use the action research process of (1) gathering data, (2) analyzing the data, and (3) providing a feedback presentation for those from whom the data were collected. When the client accepts this approach, it is understood that we will present our report orally.

The purpose of presenting the data orally is that it provides a collaborative environment for the clients to self-diagnose and commit to action. Following this presentation, we revise the notes we took during the meeting and summarize the recommendations and findings in a written report. As OD practitioners, we use data as a means to uncover issues, and the report, while maintaining anonymity, is intended to energize clients around the data and purposefully engage them in developing recommendations and action plans.

If during contract discussions the client indicates that we are expected to supply a written report, we write a brief and concise summary of our findings before we present them orally. However, we always review the report in a face-to-face meeting with the client and collaboratively decide the best method for delivering the results to the employees who contributed to the data gathering process.

Whether oral or written, our reports are easy to understand and should encourage people in the organization to say "This is what we are saying about ourselves, we believe the data represent reality, and we want to do something to change or improve the current situation."

OBJECTIVES OF THE PRESENTATION

Whether the presentation is for a single person or a group of 200, the overall goals are pretty much the same. The members of the audience want to answer several questions:

- Why was the study conducted? What was the purpose of the assignment? What did the client want to find out? Why was it important to obtain this information?
- How were the data collected: Who was interviewed? Who was surveyed? What records were reviewed?
- How were the data analyzed?
- What were the major findings? Why are these findings important?

However, presentations offer an opportunity to do far more than just summarize the data. After all, most clients are perfectly capable of reading the report to get that information. Rather, an on-site presentation gives you an opportunity to ensure not only that the client understands the findings and is satisfied with the process that was used to gather the data but also that the client understands the benefits that will accrue to the company (or unit) if the recommended actions are implemented.

MAKING EFFECTIVE PRESENTATIONS

As with the other elements in a consulting project, making a successful presentation is not difficult so long as you follow a few time-honored recommendations. Table 7.1 divides the process in to six basic steps.

TABLE 7.1
Six Steps for Making Effective Presentations

1. Ask the client or group whether the feedback report is clear.
2. Ask whether any data are missing.
3. Ask the client or group members to describe any trends they see emerging from the data. Discuss these trends in some detail.
4. Ask what actions the client or group members envision occurring in response to the data.
5. Discuss the logic and reasoning behind the actions you have recommended.
6. Promote the value of, and assist the client in, taking action.

1. *Ask the client or group whether the feedback report is clear.* It is always a good idea at the beginning of a consultant–client presentation to clarify whether the client and other people at the meeting understand the goal of the research you were brought in to do and the overall research findings. Sometimes this requires some fairly serious probing. You will want to avoid embarking on further discussion until everyone is on the same page about why you were hired and the questions, as you understood them, that you addressed.

2. *Ask whether any data are missing.* Should other questions have been asked and answered? Should other sources of data been pursued? Should individuals have been interviewed who were overlooked? Alternatively, should data have been looked at from another perspective—for example, sales by market segment rather than by geographical region? What, if any, further analysis would clarify the issues under discussion?

3. *Ask the client or group members if they see any trends emerging from the data.* As people mention trends, be sure to discuss them in some detail. Discussion is often lively as the group begins to take ownership of the data and identify actions to be taken.

4. *Ask what actions the client or group members envision occurring in response to the data.* On the basis of the discussion thus far and, perhaps, conclusions the meeting participants reached from reading the feedback report, what actions should the organization take to address its problem/challenge? These recommendations should be listed and discussed.

5. *Discuss the logic and reasoning behind the actions you recommended.* Each recommendation should be fully discussed, including the value and the potential drawbacks of taking each action. Group members should be encouraged to suggest other ways to approach the issue under discussion.

6. *Promote the value of, and assist the client in, taking action.* Before wrapping up the meeting, ask the participants whether they feel comfortable accepting the recommendations (either yours or those generated by the group) and implementing the agreed-on actions. Sometimes clients suggest moving ahead with minor changes. At other times, the group accepts some of the recommendations and decides to hold decision on others pending further study. Finally, sometimes the group is not ready to accept any of the recommendations. In this case, you will probably want to explore why the group is so reluctant to follow through and how to overcome this resistance.

If you follow the agenda outlined here, lively, valuable discussion and debate should ensue. Covering these six points as thoroughly as necessary may even require several meetings and getting together with several groups from within the client organization. At the very least, by following this agenda you can be assured that the client will develop a good grasp not only of the problem(s) facing the organization but also of possible solutions. Equally important, this process builds ownership and commitment to the actions that will take place.

In the next section you will read a case study involving a shoe manufacturer that we introduced in chapter 4. All the events actually happened; all that have been changed are the names of the manufacturer and the consulting company. After reading the case and the discussion, you should have a much better understanding of the dynamics of feedback meetings. Note in particular the strategy the consultant and the contact at the client organization used to present the research findings and, once the findings were accepted, to move the company to action.

CASE STUDY

Extra Income or Needless Work?

In chapter 4, we briefly discussed the case of XtraComfort Shoes. Our focus in that chapter was in deciding how to collect the necessary information that would answer the client's questions on whether to sell the company's products on the Internet. In this chapter, we assume that the data have been collected and that the question now is how to present the data to the client in a way that will move the client to action. To refresh your memory, we begin with a review of the company and the consultant's assignment.

XtraComfort Shoes, as its name suggests, specializes in very comfortable footwear. Established in 1972, the company has a solid market of loyal customers. XtraComfort's major retail outlets have been major department stores in the United States and a declining number of independent shoe stores.

The explosion in the use of the Internet as a forum for retailers to sell merchandise has led top management at XtraComfort to consider opening a virtual shoe store. With the approval of the executive team, the vice president of marketing and sales has engaged the services of a consulting firm called Consulting Experts, which specializes in marketing and selling on the Web. Among the specific questions XtraComfort wants answered are the following: What are the long-term prospects for companies selling on the Internet? What advantages would there be for XtraComfort if it moved into this market? What costs would XtraCost incur if it sold its shoes over the Internet? What would its 5-year sales and profit numbers look like? What does the consulting firm recommend XtraComfort do concerning this issue?

Consulting Experts conducted a complete analysis of XtraComfort's current and potential customers, its competitors, the costs and structure needed to set up an Internet-based retail division, and sales projections if it were to do so. In preparing its diagnosis and analysis, Consulting Experts followed closely the principles presented in chapter 4. Also as recommended, many internal stakeholders were involved in conducting the research and analysis, bearing in mind that these folks would be significantly involved if the company moved to Web-based retail.

Having answered XtraComfort's questions, Consulting Experts wrote a report using the format outlined in chapter 6. Given the scope of the project, the report consisted of two parts. The first part contained a summary of the consultants' findings and recommendations. The second part (actually a separate document) contained a more detailed analysis of the data on which the conclusions were based.

The question the consultants faced at this juncture was how to present the research findings most effectively. They rejected immediately the possibility of simply mailing the client the report. They also rejected the idea of dropping off the report at XtraComfort's office. Both options were clearly poor consulting practices. Either method would not have accomplished the consultants' primary objectives—that is, assisting the client in understanding the data, answering the client's questions or concerns, finding out whether further data collection or analyses would be helpful, and assisting the client in taking action.

So, what did the consultants do instead? First, they realized that if Xtra-Comfort were going to implement Consulting Experts' recommendations, several levels of review would be needed. Working with their primary client—the vice president of sales and marketing—the consultants decided to present their data in a series of meetings at XtraComfort's headquarters.

At the first meeting, the consultants presented the report, clearly labeled "draft," to the vice president of sales and marketing and two of her key associates. This meeting took almost a full day. The goal was to systematically go through what the consulting firm had done, what data had been collected, why they were collected, and how they were presented in the report. Throughout the meeting, the firm received feedback on the client's reaction to the work, including additional information that needed to be collected, issues or problems the client saw as highlighted in the data, and how the conclusions could be presented more effectively. The consultants did not present their recommendations at this meeting; they had decided in advance that the focus at this point would be on ensuring that the consultants had collected all the information the client thought was necessary to decide whether to open a virtual store.

After the first meeting, the consultants followed up on the client's suggestion and collected additional information. After revising their written report, they then presented their major findings to about 20 members of the marketing and sales staff in a half-day session. The agenda for this meeting followed the agenda suggested at the beginning of this chapter. First, the consultants described the purpose of their study. Second, they talked about how the data were collected. Third, they reviewed the major findings. Fourth and finally, they recommended that XtraComfort open an Internet store and the reasons they had reached that decision. Throughout this meeting, the consultants solicited questions and suggestions from the 20 members of the group.

A few days later, several key people in the marketing and sales department met to review the consultants' report again. This time, the consultants were not present. Those in attendance voted to endorse the decision to set up an Internet retail store, taking into account some of the changes that the consultants had recommended.

Next, a list of the recommendations of the marketing and sales group, together with the consultants' report, was distributed to officers and units in the company that would potentially be affected by the creation of an online store. Two of these units expressed concerns and discussed these in meetings with the marketing people. The consultants were present at these meetings to answer questions.

Finally, the recommendations were presented to XtraComfort's executive team. The company's marketing and salespeople did most of the talking, while the consultants served more as resources when questions arose. The executive team supported the recommendations with minor changes.

The CEO then presented the recommendations to the board of directors, which approved the plan as outlined. The recommendations were implemented, and XtraComfort now has a very successful online store.

Implications

Although this case study provides only a brief snapshot of the process by which the consultants presented their findings to XtraComfort, it illustrates the importance of having a well-designed strategy for making presentations. Had the consultants just handed the report to the vice president, who knows what would have happened? Probably not much, at least initially, while the client tried to figure out what to do next.

By working with the client to ensure that the key players at XtraComfort had the information and analyses they needed, the consultants ensured that the client was both well informed and able to make an intelligent decision. Had the evidence indicated that an Internet store was not a prudent decision, XtraComfort's sales and marketing team could have made an equally informed decision not to pursue Internet selling. Equally important, even with this scenario, the consultants would have provided value for the money by preventing the company from embarking on a losing strategy, thereby enabling XtraComfort to focus on more promising marketing initiatives.

PRINCIPLES OF EFFECTIVE RESEARCH PRESENTATIONS

Most consultants work on extremely varied projects, so that no single presentation strategy fits all situations. However, you can certainly increase the probability of a successful outcome simply by following some helpful principles, which are outlined in Table 7.2.

Remember the Objective

Sometimes consultants get sidetracked with irrelevant issues, such as trying to impress a client with their expertise. It is critical to keep the goal of the consulting assignment in mind, whether you are writing a feedback report or presenting research findings—that is, to assist the client in taking action. The purpose of the presentation is to move the client or the organization closer to achieving this goal. The focus, therefore, should always be on moving the client in this direction.

Use the Report as a Basis for Action

The client knows the culture and politics of the organization and how to get things done. Before preparing the report in final form, and before mak-

---

TABLE 7.2
Tips for Making Effective Research Presentations

- Always remember the overall objective.
- Use the feedback report as a basis for action.
- Be sure every meeting has a purpose and an agenda.
- Make sure key people are at the meeting(s).
- Allow plenty of time.
- Facilitate, don't pontificate.
- Engage the client in both conducting research and taking action.
- Don't get defensive! See challenges to the report as an opportunity to understand the clients' issues and concerns.
- Move to action!
- Always know the next step.

---

ing a presentation, you and the client should map out a strategy for presenting the report and then getting the organization to act on its recommendations.

Be Sure Meetings Have a Purpose and Agenda

Meetings with only vague goals and no agendas are usually disasters. Every meeting should be carefully planned. What is the purpose of the meeting? What outcomes are desired? How should the meeting be structured to deliver that outcome? The client and the consultant need to agree on the answers to these questions, which means they need to plan each meeting together.

Also important to the success of a meeting, and ultimately to the success of a consulting project, is ensuring that the individuals in attendance understand the purpose of the meeting and know the agenda. It is difficult to be an active participant at a meeting if you don't have a clear idea of the reason you are there or what's on the agenda or, worse, if the purpose and agenda are kept secret.

Be Sure Key People Attend

As in the case of the purpose and agenda, you and the client must agree on who in the organization has power and authority. You may want to ask the client such questions as "Who needs to know the information in the report?", "Who can take action on the recommendations?", "Whose approval is needed to take action?", and "Who would be affected if the recommendations were acted on?" The people whose names are mentioned must be at the meeting when you present your research findings. Otherwise, you are likely to waste time talking to people who have little or no authority. Equally problematic, if the key players in the organization are not at the meeting, the participants may not be motivated to actively contribute or have the knowledge to critique the findings in the report as rigorously as is needed to make the meeting, and, ultimately, the project, a success.

Allow Plenty of Time

One occasionally hears of a consultant who was "allowed 10 minutes" at a management meeting to report the results of a 9-month study and analysis. When we hear of this, alarm bells ring for several reasons. Most obviously, if management thinks the study is worthy of only 10 minutes of management's time, then one has to wonder whether the study was worth undertaking to begin with. Assuming the study was worth the effort, 10 minutes is simply not enough time to do justice to a report on the findings.

As we have said, to commit the client to action, the client, and typically several key people in the client organization, must thoroughly understand the data collection method, the research findings, and the implications and recommendations discussed in the report. Not only are 10 minutes nowhere near enough time to discuss this amount of material, but also two or more meetings of several hours each may be necessary. In the case discussed earlier, for example, the consultants presented their findings over several meetings. Furthermore, the consultant may need to meet separately with various groups. The point to remember is that you and the client need to devise a strategy for conducting the meeting and have sufficient time to present and discuss the findings.

Facilitate, Don't Pontificate

Your role at the presentation is to serve more as a facilitator than as an expert presenter. Granted, much of the meeting may be focused on presenting the results of the report, but the meeting should be more than (in consultants' language) a "data dump." Moving the client to action often requires considerable skill as a facilitator.

Engage the Client

By addressing several questions touched on earlier in this chapter, you should be able to encourage the client, as well as the others at the presentation, to begin to take ownership of the project:

- Are the data presented clearly?
- Are additional data needed. If so, what additional data?
- How do those at the meeting interpret the data?
- Does anyone have reservations about the progress of the work so far?
- What trends do they see emerging from the data? What strikes them as most important?

By the end of the presentation, you should have moved the client and the others at the meeting to action. One way to facilitate this is by asking what actions they think need to be taken. Many consultants find it useful to brainstorm possibilities and have the group identify the actions they think would be most effective.

Don't Get Defensive!

Clients often raise questions about feedback reports. Managers have also been known to challenge the study itself, to the point of asking why the organization wasted its money on conducting the research. They may not understand why a particular group was surveyed, or why some other group was not. They may question specific analyses or challenge the validity of conclusions and recommendations. Consultants come across as far more professional and effective if they strive to clarify the client's issues and concerns rather than react defensively. The best approach under such stressful circumstances is to try not to take the criticism personally and to answer the questions the best way possible. Inevitably, someone wants more detail, while someone else is perfectly satisfied with less. In other words, it rarely is possible to satisfy everybody. Remember, the people who challenge a study the most loudly often have little or no knowledge of why or how the study was conducted.

If the research, data collection, and analysis were well designed and approved by the client, you should be able to respond effectively to most challenges. Bear in mind, however, that there is no such thing as a perfect study or a perfect report. At times you may have to acknowledge that you could have collected additional data or performed additional analyses but that, given the constraints of time or money, you had to make difficult choices.

Move to Action!

We cannot emphasize enough that the purpose of a consulting assignment is to assist the client organization in becoming more effective. Sometimes the best action is inaction; in the case of XtraComfort, for example, management might have concluded, based on the consultants' findings, that setting up an Internet store was a poor business decision. The point is that an effective consultant is one who provides all the information and advice the client needs to make a deliberate, well-thought-out decision that will enhance the organization's strength and viability overall.

What's the Next Step?

You and the client should end every meeting with a plan concerning the next step. Thus, every meeting should end with a decision about who will do what, by when, in response to each of the major points discussed at the meeting. Specifically, an action plan should be generated in writing that details what will happen next and who will take various actions.

PRESENTATION STRATEGIES

Although the 10 principles for effective presentation of a report will lead to more successful consulting, it is important to remember that there is no one way of making an effective presentation. The client's needs and expectations always have to be taken into account. Consider, for example, the techniques used in each of the following three cases.

Case 1: XYZ and the Job Satisfaction Survey

The vice president of human resources at XYZ Inc., a company with approximately 7,000 employees, contracted with a survey research firm to conduct XYZ's biannual job satisfaction survey. The consultants assisted XYZ in designing the survey, administering it, tabulating the results, and presenting the results in a report. The only presentation the consultants made was for the purpose of demonstrating that the research firm had complied with XYZ's survey specifications. The members of the human resources unit at XYZ interpreted the results themselves, made recommendations, and gave presentations to the key managers in the company.

Case 2: The Central Region Service Center

As you may recall, in chapter 6 we discussed a regional service center that had recently gone through restructuring. The board of directors asked a consulting firm to interview employees about how well the restructuring had gone as well as what, if any, issues were still unresolved. After interviewing a representative group of employees, the consultants summarized their findings in the report shown at the end of chapter 6.

The consultants first presented the findings in the report at an informal meeting with the center director and a couple of the key staff from the center. These staff were aware of most of the issues the employees had raised and had already been thinking of ways to rectify the problems. Together, the consultants and the staff members reached a consensus regarding which recommendations to undertake.

The consultants then presented the report and the agreed-on recommendations at a meeting of the board of directors. Each board member was given a copy of the report, which contained summaries of each point discussed in the meeting as well as the consultants' recommendations. Few questions were raised about the report's content. On a couple of occasions, the president of the board asked the center director if he thought the report was accurate. The director said that he thought it was and that the center planned to implement the recommendations fairly quickly.

The board voted to accept the report and its recommendations and ordered the center director to begin making the changes the consultants recommended.

In this case, what moved the client quickly to action was that the consultants and the staff of the center collaborated well in developing the recommended actions. Furthermore, the client (the board) seemed to accept the consultants' analysis and recommendations at face value; the board expressed no interest in becoming involved in discussion of the issues or the recommendations. From presentation of the recommendations to approval probably took no more than 20 minutes.

Case 3: The Medical Center Management Committee

Because of considerable tension among the members of the management committee of a large medical center, the CEO hired a consultant to help the committee resolve several disagreements. The consultant interviewed the members of the committee and identified seven issues that seemed to be major points of conflict. For example, one issue, which had been discussed for more than a year, was whether to purchase a medical helicopter.

After the interviews were conducted, the consultant and the committee had a day-long meeting offsite. The consultant did not present a written report; instead, she wrote each of the seven issues she had identified on a flip chart, briefly described each one, and asked for confirmation from the group that her descriptions were accurate. She did not draw any conclusions (other than that she had identified the seven issues), and she did not make any recommendations about actions or changes the committee should make. However, each issue was discussed at length during the meeting.

Perhaps not surprisingly, an underlying issue (as discussed in chap. 4) emerged that related to all seven issues under discussion. Specifically, several members of the committee thought that the CEO of the medical center was too indecisive and was causing many of the problems the members of the committee had identified. As an example, they pointed to his indecision surrounding the helicopter. The CEO countered that he did not have a medical degree and looked to the medical staff for guidance on decisions requiring medical knowledge. Because the medical staff could not agree on whether to purchase the helicopter, the issue had languished. Members of the committee countered that medical staffs typically consist of rather strong-willed individuals who rarely are in complete agreement about anything; in the face of conflicting viewpoints, it was the CEO's obligation to make a decision. The CEO said he better understood what was expected of him and would fulfill his responsibilities. (The medical center purchased the helicopter the following week.)

Without belaboring an obvious point, these examples illustrate how the consultant's presentation strategy needs to vary depending on the client's expectations and requirements. In the first case, the client did not want a presentation. Once the consultants had prepared the survey, the client simply wanted data on the job satisfaction levels of the company's employees and to know that the survey had been conducted according to the specifications the company requested.

In the second case, the consultant presented the results to key staff and, together with the consultant, developed (achievable) recommendations. Subsequently, the board of directors was presented with the consultant's report, which also contained the recommendations for action. These recommendations were accepted without question, and the board ordered the director to implement them at once.

Finally, in the third case, the consultant did not even prepare a written report. The seven issues she identified were listed on a flip chart, and she facilitated a discussion of each. To the consultant's credit, she picked up on a broad underlying issue that was raised at the meeting. Ultimately, this issue was resolved together with the seven issues related to it.

OTHER DETAILS TO BEAR IN MIND

A variety of additional questions often arise with regard to making client presentations. For example, should the consultant use PowerPoint slides, overheads, or flip charts? Who should receive copies of the report? Should the consultant allow the client to see the report before the official presentation? Should the consultant allow the client to change parts of the report, such as conclusions or recommendations, prior to its official release?

Probably the best advice is that consultants and clients should decide together how best to present their findings. As for the last question—whether the consultant should allow the client to change parts of the report—the answer is only if the change enhances the validity of the findings or the overall clarity. To alter findings is a violation of consulting ethics.

SUMMARY

Presentation of your research findings and recommendations is another critical part of the consulting process. Following the success factors listed next will greatly increase the likelihood that you will achieve your ultimate objective: motivating the client to implement your recommendations.

KEY SUCCESS FACTORS FOR PRESENTING STUDY FINDINGS

- Remember that the objective of the consulting assignment is to assist the client in taking action and that the longer term goal is to increase the effectiveness of the client organization. The presentation strategy should reflect both these objectives.
- Work with the client in developing the presentation strategy. The client knows the culture and politics of the organization better than an outsider, and knows how to get things done.
- Plan meetings carefully. Every meeting should have a purpose and an agenda.
- Allow plenty of time, and make sure the key people are at the meetings.
- Function as a facilitator in the meetings rather than just summarizing the report.
- Engage the client. Foster ownership of the issues and data under discussion.
- Encourage participants at the meeting(s) to offer their insights and opinions. Help them move to action.
- Don't get defensive. See challenges to the report as opportunities to understand issues affecting the client organization.
- Keep moving the client to action. The design of the presentation strategy should ensure that every step assists the client in moving forward.
- Always include "next steps." Every meeting should end with a decision about follow-up, including who does what, when.

8

Initiating Action

Once the data collection phase of a consulting project is over and the client has decided to initiate some type of change, the part that many consultants consider the most rewarding—the implementation or execution stage—can begin. This is when real change occurs. In some cases, this change is evident only in a unit or department. In other cases, it is organization wide. Regardless, the implementation stage is when the talking ceases and concrete action or intervention starts in earnest.

Even when the results of the consultant's study are extremely convincing, executing action in response to the findings is rarely easy, whether the unit involved is a small division or an entire company. In this chapter we discuss strategies for implementing action or change effectively.

As in every phase of the project, questions need to be answered, and steps taken, before action can be initiated. We therefore begin by discussing the planning that needs to take place before implementation can begin. Throughout the chapter, a case study is used to illustrate key points.

PLANNING THE ACTION

Defining Your Role

Throughout this book, we have emphasized the need, at each stage of a project, for the consultant, the contact at the client organization, and other key players in the company to agree on the consultant's role. Are you going to be an active participant in the project or more of an outside expert/adviser? Addressing this question is as important during the implementation phase as at any other stage of a project. There is a tendency among some consultants, for example, to become surrogate managers. They want to take over and make all the decisions. They act as if they know what is best for the organization (after all, didn't they collect the data?) and therefore should be totally in charge of whatever action or change takes place. Other consultants take the opposite approach. They recede into the background, suggesting that now that the data collection and diagnosis phase is over, so is their involvement in the project. Neither of these approaches is effective. Maintaining a balance of power and sharing control are as critical now as at other stages of the project.

Ideally, you and the client should both be actively involved as implementation of change occurs. In some cases, this means that you may be more actively involved than at any other phase of the project. In other cases, you may have to relinquish some ownership of the recommendations for action.

Forming a Planning Team

Let's assume for a moment that you have been brought in to the Willis Auto Supply Company to help improve the time it takes to ship products to customers. On the basis of research you have conducted, including interviews, questionnaires, and observation, you and the client have zeroed in on the division that manufactures hubcaps as one in which production delays are common. Delays are far less common in other divisions in the company, and when delays do happen, the effects are much less serious. In the long term, Willis would like to fully automate its production lines, and the Willis executives see the hubcaps division as a good place to start.

You and the client discuss how to proceed and decide that you will form a planning team, which Willis refers to as a *task force*, consisting of several managers and employees who are very knowledgeable about the production process and who have good planning skills. The task force's charge is to plan in some detail all the changes that will occur throughout Willis so that any changes are implemented will proceed as smoothly as possible.

In general, such a planning team should include all the key players or representatives of the departments affected by the recommended changes. Among the people invited at Willis Auto Supply are people from several units, including purchasing, training, and accounts payable, as well as the head of the hubcaps division and other people in manufacturing. Inviting well-respected people of influence and authority is important. The changes being proposed may directly affect their work areas as well as the company as a whole.

In general, a planning team should have between 5 and 15 people. Eliciting a diversity of ideas is valuable and often not possible if the group is too small. At the same time, the team should not be so big as to make in-depth discussion difficult or make it likely that a few members of the team will dominate. Sometimes it is useful to invite a larger group to the first meeting and split into two or small subcommittees later on.

Initial Meeting

To get back to our case study, a memo is circulated at Willis alerting the members of the task force that an initial meeting will be held. In addition to the people mentioned earlier, you and the client invite top management, although the assumption is that not all of them will remain on the team or attend future meetings.

Three general objectives are set forth for the initial meeting:

1. Determine the purpose of the implementation phase of the project. What should be accomplished?
2. Clarify the task force's charge or directive. What is expected of the team members? What is the team expected to accomplish? What is the timeline?
3. Decide on the tasks that need to be accomplished as well as who will be responsible for each task.

You and the client agree that you will facilitate the meeting, but the client will actively participate.

To Train or Not to Train?

It is not uncommon after a planning committee or task force is formed for the consultant and client to decide that the members need training before they can work together successfully. The focus of the training, which in some cases can take several days or more, is typically on the development of team-building and/or project management skills.

As part of the training, some planning committees develop an operating agreement or code of conduct. This agreement specifies how the team will conduct its business as well as how the members of the team will interact with each other. This becomes the list of rules the team will live by. These rules are often written on a large sheet of paper that each member of the team must sign. Table 8.1 shows a working agreement that the members of the task force at Willis Auto Supply might have been asked to sign.

Creating a Vision

Reaching agreement on the goals everyone hopes to achieve is critical to success at the implementation phase of a project. During the initial meet-

TABLE 8.1
Rules for Working Together

- All team members will attend all task force meetings, on time.
- All members will freely share their opinions and ideas. We are working as a collaborative team—"bosses" are not allowed.
- We will respect everyone's ideas and suggestions.
- All members will be kept informed of all actions being taken. Communication will be open.
- The content of all our discussions will remain confidential—what is said by task force members stays with task force members. Communication with people who are not on this task force should be through official channels.
- No "bitching" is allowed—we will spend our energy figuring how to get things done, not complaining about why they have not gotten done in the past.

---

ing at Willis Auto Supply, for example, the members of the task force reviewed the recommendations you discussed in detail in the research report, about how the company should address the delays in the hubcaps division. In the report, you noted that the equipment used in hubcaps was older than other equipment in the company and operated more slowly, so that it was more likely to break down and need to be repaired. Your conclusion, stated in your report, was that, in combination, these problems had set in motion a cycle of delays and frustration.

With assistance from Willis engineers and managers, you recommended that the production process in the hubcaps division needed to be made fully automated, the production process redesigned to accommodate the new procedures, and the employees retrained in how to operate the new equipment. In addition to recommending these changes, you suggested a possible design for the new automated system as well as a vendor who could provide the new equipment. According to your estimates, acceptance of these recommendations would allow Willis to increase production by more than 700% per hour and cut the cost per unit produced by 30%. Subsequently, Willis's management endorsed your recommendations and committed financial resources to the project.

Thus, the overall vision of the task force is to implement a fully automated production process in the hubcaps division, as well as all necessary support services, such as just-in-time inventory. Willis's engineers and managers have projected that the fully automated process could be operational within 6 months.

The participants at the initial meeting of the task force decide that more planning is necessary before implementation of the changes can begin. Specifically, they need to know the cost of the equipment that you are recommending; when the equipment could be delivered; the services the equipment vendor provides to its customers; and the time and training required to get some or all of the members of the hubcaps division up to speed on using the equipment, including the software. Someone suggests that perhaps a benchmarking study should be conducted with an eye toward seeing how companies using similar systems have fared.

A subcommittee is formed to analyze how best to obtain all the data the company needs. Just before wrapping up the meeting, you and the client reinforce that significant, perhaps unanticipated, changes could occur as a result of the actions being proposed for the hubcaps division. Consequently, you both emphasize that although everyone is eager to see results, careful consideration needs to be given to the implications of the changes. Finally, everyone agrees on a date by which the subcommittee will report back, and the meeting is adjourned.

Conducting a Stakeholder Analysis

As part of the process of assessing the pros and cons of taking recommended actions, a planning committee will sometimes undertake what is called a *stakeholder analysis*. A stakeholder analysis usually has two parts. The first part involves identifying all the parties who will be affected by the proposed change. It identifies exactly who will have to do things differently as well as what type of changes they will experience. In the case discussed here, one such group would be the very people on whom implementation is focused: the members of the hubcaps division. Any time new equipment is introduced, work routines change, along with expectations about productivity, skills, and so forth. Furthermore, introducing automation often means that some employees will have to be reassigned or let go.

The second part of the stakeholder analysis focuses on ensuring that all of the key stakeholders are on board with the changes being proposed. It is the planning committee's responsibility to explain the importance of the changes to the stakeholders, to understand and address their concerns, and to elicit their support. Receiving the full support of the organization's key players that the changes being recommended are necessary and in the organization's best interests is a major step toward implementing a successful project.

Realistically, it is often impossible to get the full support of all stakeholders, especially if their own jobs are on the line. This is not uncommon, for example, when several departments are merged. Similarly, the introduction of new technology often means that some workers may not be needed or that workers who have difficulty learning the new technology may have to be replaced. Under these circumstances, some groups are obviously not going to be supportive of the changes taking place around them. The stakeholder analysis can still be helpful in a couple of ways, however. For example, it identifies the needs of various groups, such as which employees are going to need training and which are going to need outplacement assistance. The company may not have even accounted for the fact that such needs must be met.

Creating the Project Plan

One of the most important tasks of the planning committee or task force is the development of the *project plan*. This plan details what changes will occur in the organization, the sequence in which they will occur, when they will occur, and what resources are needed to accomplish them. In short, the plan provides a step-by-step map of the change effort.

In Willis's case, the plan took several weeks to complete. Most project plans focus on a couple of key pieces. For Willis, this was the new equipment. The equipment had to be customized to meet Willis's specifications, and delivery dates had to be established.

Setting up training was another key piece in the undertaking. Several employees and supervisors at Willis received some initial training at a noncompetitor's facility, but most of the training was conducted after the equipment was in place.

Once the plan for change has been written, it has to be collated and put into a usable form. Many consultants present all the data in notebooks (with a good table of contents so that the information can easily be found).

Willis's final project plan was put on a computer file and consisted of process flow charts, Gantt charts, responsibility matrices, organizational charts, and diagrams. The computer file was made easily accessible to each team member. This enabled everyone not only to view the plan, as well as the new production line, but also to raise questions to which anyone could respond.

There is no such thing as a perfect plan. At some point, everyone has to agree to forge ahead. As much as possible, however, the emphasis should be on developing detailed plans while ensuring flexibility and allowing for contingencies. Also, although it is important that deadlines be outlined and milestones identified, it also is important to have a backup plan ready should unforeseen events occur—for example, in the case of Willis, if the equipment does not arrive on the promised date.

Presenting the Plan

Because enlisting upper management's support for a change is so critical, after the stakeholder analysis and other studies have been conducted, the consultant and client will frequently invite top management to a meeting at which all the data are presented. The focus should be on presenting a clear, quantitative summary of the data. The overall goal of this meeting is to convince top management of the value of proceeding. Several key points that need to be covered at this meeting are noted in Table 8.2.

Receiving Approval and Resources

The final step in the planning stage is when top management gives the go-ahead to proceed. At this point, top management should be willing to allocate the resources necessary for the projected change(s), including money, personnel, and equipment. Receiving approval is critical; without the tangible resources, the implementation phase can never be successful. Likewise, key people in the organization need to support not only the need for action but also the specific actions to be taken.

Turning Resistance Into Acceptance

Returning to our case study, let's assume that the company has decided to go ahead and order the new equipment for the hubcaps division and arrange to train several people in how to use it. At a subsequent meeting, which you attend along with the client and key members of the company,

TABLE 8.2
Key Points to Address With Top Management

- What is the specific problem that needs to be addressed?
- Why is it a problem?
- What is the strategy for improvement?
- What will be the benefits of effecting change?
- What are the execution costs?
- How will action be executed (who will be involved, when, what are the start and completion dates, etc.)?
- Include any questions that would be of particular importance to the company. For example, in Willis's case, top management was concerned about losing production time. Thus, the transition from the old system to the new had to be made very quickly.

several people express concern that there is likely to be some serious resistance to the changes planned for hubcaps. Among the challenges are convincing several rank-and-file workers that adapting to the changes in the division is in the best interests of the workers.

In Willis's case, the resistance was from the workers. It is not uncommon, however, for consultants to encounter resistance from upper as well as middle and lower management. The long-term benefits to the organization of implementing a change in procedure, restructuring a division—or, as in this case, investing money for equipment and training—may not be readily apparent. As in our example, giving up traditions and ways of doing things can be extremely difficult, whether the changes affect a group of blue collar workers or managers at the highest levels. Regardless of where the resistance is encountered, breaking through it is critical to the successful implementation of changes.

One of the first steps in managing resistance is to understand its cause. One frequent cause is a fear of job loss or status. That could well have been a concern among the people in the hubcaps unit. They may also have had doubts whether the new way of doing things would work or work better. The manager of hubcaps may have feared losing control of or authority over his department or that he was being personally blamed for the delays in his department. He may also have become concerned that he would no longer have the skills or ability to manage once the changes were implemented. By following some basic guidelines, you can play an important role in helping managers and other personnel overcome resistance. Some key points to bear in mind when trying to counter this common reaction to changes are listed in Table 8.3.

Educating everyone affected about whatever changes are taking place is critical to breaking down resistance and, ultimately, to implementing ac-

TABLE 8.3
Countering Resistance to Change

- Treat the resistance seriously. Try to understand the underlying causes of the resistance and to address it head on.

- Encourage the client or a key contact person in the organization to provide several opportunities throughout the implementation process for individuals who are resistant to the changes to explore their concerns.

- Communicate openly and honestly about the changes taking place. No one wants to be left in the dark about what is happening.

- Encourage those affected by the changes to provide suggestions of ways to implement the changes in the least disruptive way possible. Ideally, this should break down resistance while advancing project goals.

- Don't take resistance personally.

tions effectively. People must understand why changes are taking place to embrace them. They also need to understand that the company is going to make every effort to place the current employees in either the new production line or in comparable jobs.

EXECUTING ACTION

Forming the Implementation Team

At the beginning of the action stage, another team should be formed to focus on implementation. Ideally, this team should consist of the same people who were on the planning committee, although it may be advisable to replace some team members and substitute others. At Willis Auto Supply, rank-and-file members of the hubcaps division might be added to the team, especially if they promote the value of the action and are well respected by their peers. Including such people as team members provides a direct link to the workers most affected and therefore to learning workers' reactions to the changes. In addition, workers directly affected by the changes can be valuable in helping others in the division or department recognize the value of the action taking place.

As with the planning team, the implementation team may need training. Even if the members of the team have had training in the skills they'll need, they are likely to benefit from a short course either to review some of the basics or on a more advanced topic, such as conflict management.

Likewise, the team members may be weak in project management. There are many software programs for help in this area; however, be sure the system is not so complex as to confuse the team members.

Selling the Project

One of the important duties of the implementation team is to sell the project. By the time the planning team has finished its work, there will be plenty of rumors floating around about the change effort, and typically people will be more focused on the potential negative impact of the changes than on positive outcomes. To counteract the rumors and keep people informed, the implementation team will need to work hard to "sell" the project. Team members will need to emphasize the positive benefits of the project while not denying that the change may disrupt some current routines. There are a variety of strategies available to accomplish this goal. Some project teams hold one-on-one meetings with key managers to make sure they are on board. In unionized settings, they may also hold several meetings with union officials to inform them about the purpose and details of the project.

Another strategy teams use is to have a project kickoff ceremony to which all employees are invited. At Willis Auto Supply, for example, top executives might have spoken at such a ceremony about the importance of the changes to Willis's future, including how they would allow the company to remain competitive with other auto suppliers and ensure that Willis's doors would remain open. The executives would also want to assure employees that their jobs weren't in jeopardy. Finally, the project team would want to be sure to outline the details of the project and answer questions.

The manner in which the project is "sold," and who is responsible for communicating the details about it, varies for each project and organization. What is important is that you should never assume that the benefits of change will be immediately apparent to managers or employees. Many managers and employees have not been part of the discovery and decision process and have to be convinced of the positive aspects of the changes that will occur.

Communicate, Communicate, Communicate!

As noted earlier, changes often arouse great anxiety, confusion, and rumors (some of which are false or bizarre). Constant communication throughout the project is the key to dispelling the rumors and confusion. It is not possible to overcommunicate during a change effort.

In this chapter's "From the Expert ..." section, Richard Bailey discusses the importance to the success of a project of communicating and sharing information. As Bailey reminds us, everyone should be informed of the reasons for a change project and understand the project plan, including what will be happening and when. He also claims that everyone needs to understand the procedures in place if retraining is necessary, as well as arrangements that are being made for employees who are being terminated. For Bailey, communicating change is a key factor to a successful change initiative.

At Willis, many of the plans were discussed at the kickoff ceremony. Plans were also posted on a special bulletin board, and periodic briefings were held for management-level employees as well as for union officers. A special Web site was set up that included the plans, progress reports, and a hotline through which employees could ask questions; questions and answers were posted for all to see.

Willis's communication strategy was to use multiple channels of communication. Most change efforts involve such a strategy. In some cases, employees rely on the information provided by their supervisors. In other cases, they don't trust the supervisor and want communication to be in writing, and in still other cases, they rely on the word of their union steward only.

From the Experts ...
A Few Simple Steps to Implement Change
by Richard E. Bailey
Bailey Consulting

I have worked in operations for more than 35 years and have had my share of successes when implementing change in organizations. Implementing change isn't easy; in fact, it's very, very hard. But by following a few simple steps, you can increase the probability of success in any organization.

The key to a successful change effort is the change team. The team members must believe in the change in order to sell the change to others. You must also establish targets that demonstrate the positive outcomes that will result. You must then inform everyone about the change in a meaningful way and establish incentives that motivate employees to embrace the change wholeheartedly. Finally, you must have a systematic follow-up plan that provides useful feedback and continues to encourage employees to follow through with the change effort.

When implementing change, it's often easy to slip back into old and bad habits. This all boils down to five principles that I always use to guide me when change is critical:

1. Select your team carefully. Team members must be leaders who believe in what you believe in.

2. Establish new targets that demonstrate "if you do what you have always done, you will get what you have always gotten." Results from the past are not good enough; targets need to be an extreme stretch.

3. Communicate, communicate, communicate. From the top person down, people need to market why change is critical.

4. Establish incentives that allow all to share in the organization's success. Financial rewards as well as small token "attaboys" are all critical.

5. Follow-up and visibility are critical. Track results and give feedback to everyone in the organization on a regular basis. During the implementation stage, sharing data and information is essential to success.

MONITORING PROGRESS

You, the client, and the implementation team should meet regularly to monitor progress during implementation. This is a good idea for several reasons. First, problems can be identified and corrective action taken. Second, assuming that tasks have been accomplished, these meetings give everyone, from management on down, an opportunity to celebrate achievements. Third, and finally, the review process serves as a reminder of what still needs to be done and who needs to do it. If top managers do not attend these meetings, you and the planning team should probably meet regularly with some or all of these managers. It is important to keep everyone informed about accomplishments as well as delays and problems.

Yet another reason to monitor progress is that it provides a chance to fine-tune processes. Especially on larger projects, the execution stage may involve several steps, some of them elaborate. Having the option to revise not just schedules but procedures is important.

The Willis team met every Monday morning, and top management sometimes sat in on the meetings. The agenda included reviewing the project plan to assess progress and making plans for the coming week to ensure target goals were met. These meetings were very helpful in keeping the team focused.

NEED FOR FLEXIBILITY

The best of plans often are difficult to implement smoothly. Problems and changes are an inevitable part of the life of even the most successful projects. At Willis Auto Supply, several adjustments were necessary. For example, the new equipment was delivered 2 weeks earlier than scheduled. (This was highly unusual; new equipment is typically delivered from 2 weeks to 6 months late.) Because the trucks had to be unloaded and Willis had no storage facilities, the task force had to scramble to get the new equipment set up and the old equipment dismantled. Although this moved the schedule forward, negotiations with the union regarding job reclassifications—a result of the changes in production—as well as the need to outplace some workers, caused a 3-week delay in getting the new system up and running.

All change projects require adjustments. The important point is to respond effectively and forge ahead. Consultants also need to remember that, as in the agreement signed by the members of the task force, "No bitching is allowed." This may be one of the task force's most important rules.

CONGRATULATE, REWARD, AND CELEBRATE

Change efforts are often long-term projects and, as such, have their ups and downs. Studies have shown that initially there usually are a lot of energy and enthusiasm for a change effort but that energy begins to wane as problems and delays start mounting, usually a couple of months into a project. Finally, as the end is in sight, energy and enthusiasm increase to their highest level.

A great way to keep people involved and committed throughout a project is by celebrating and rewarding accomplishments. For example, in Willis's case, the company held an initial plantwide kickoff celebration. There were also celebrations as each major milestone was reached—when the new equipment was installed, for example. Another milestone was when the employees on the new line completed their training. A formal graduation ceremony was held to which families were invited and diplomas passed out, and each graduate received a small cash gift.

As each major milestone was reached, the implementation team had a brief celebration, usually a pizza lunch at a local bowling alley, but the big celebration was at the end of the project, when Willis held an open house to show off the new equipment and production line. A lot of awards were given out. In fact, the implementation team received the Willis Pioneer Award to signify that the team had taken a leadership role in Willis's efforts to automate the entire company.

SUMMARY

The action stage of a project can be the most exciting but also the most challenging. This is when you finally see the fruits of your labor: the proposal you wrote to conduct the research, the research itself, and the planning that preceded implementation. The key success factors noted next should help ensure that implementation goes smoothly, or at least at smoothly as you can hope for. Remember that making changes—whether you are the one being asked to change or you are the facilitator—is rarely easy.

KEY SUCCESS FACTORS FOR INITIATING ACTION

- Plan the change carefully. Anticipate problems and decide in advance how to handle them.
- Make sure all the key players are on board with the change.
- Make sure that the organization has allocated all the necessary resources.
- Sell the project. Make sure everyone understands the benefits of the change.
- Monitor progress and adjust in response to problems, but keep moving forward.
- Keep communication flowing. Keeping people informed about what's going to happen, who is going to be involved, and when things are going to happen is critical to success throughout a consulting project but especially during the implementation phase, when people's ways of doing things and sense of security are often threatened.
- Understand that resistance to change is natural but that it doesn't have to stand in the way of progress; it can be overcome and lead to undergoing worthwhile transitions.
- Congratulate and reward people for small as well as large accomplishments. Thank them too for jobs well done.

CHAPTER
9

Ending the Project

The old adage that endings are as important as beginnings applies to consulting projects as much as to other human endeavors. It is particularly true if you hope to create a long-term relationship with the client organization. Unfortunately, many consulting projects end too abruptly. The client and the consultant mutually decide that next Tuesday or Wednesday will be the final day of the project, or at least the last day that the consultant will be involved. The consultant then finishes up whatever can be completed by the agreed-on date, says goodbye to the client, and sends a final invoice. Ending a project in this way is not conducive to developing a lasting relationship. In this chapter we address an alternative approach in which the emphasis is on ensuring the growth of your relationships with clients in a way that is beneficial to both parties.

PLANNING THE FINAL PHASE

Ideally, the final stage of a project involves a series of activities that will ensure that the project is deemed a success and that link the current project to future assignments. These activities should also contribute to your and the client's thinking of ways you could work continue to work together.

Specifically, the goals of the final phase of the project should be to:

- Plan for the transition to the next phase of the project, if applicable, when you will not be involved.
- Celebrate the completion of the project.
- Explore how you and the client can work together even more effectively in the future by addressing such issues as your project management skills and overall working relationship.

- Explore further opportunities for collaboration.
- Secure recommendations (and referrals).
- Ensure ways to maintain a relationship.

If you achieve these goals, then successful completion of the project is likely. Moreover, the probability that you will be rehired to work on future projects is high.

KNOWING WHEN TO END

Like every other part of a consulting project, you and the client should agree on the ending date or final activities before the project even gets under way. In this chapter's "From the Experts ..." section, Elaine Patterson, a senior human resources consultant with the Unocal Corporation, reminds us why it is necessary to agree as early as possible when a project will end. For Patterson, it is important at the onset of an assignment to ask what will happen when you walk out the door. Will activities that have been started continue? Will new activities begin? Patterson claims that you and the client should discuss these questions from as early in the project as possible.

When writing up contracts, many consultants are careful to specify several activities that need to be completed at the beginning, middle, and end of the project. In addition to providing critical benchmarks to evaluate progress, using this strategy minimizes confusion about when your work is done.

PLANNING THE TRANSITION

Very often, consultants are hired to work on one or maybe a few phases of multiphased projects. One consultant might be hired to assist during installation of new software, another to design and conduct training. Or a marketing consultant might be hired to assist in identifying new markets for a company's services, and, on the basis of a study done by that consultant, another hired to help design a system to deliver those services more efficiently. Consequently, you may end up cutting your ties before a project is fully completed, leaving members of the unit or the organization to finish some of the tasks.

Such a situation could have easily happened at Willis Auto Supply, discussed in chapter 8. To refresh your memory, in that case we asked you to imagine that you were brought in to address a delivery problem, which, after several studies, was determined to involve the hubcaps division. When should or could your involvement in that project have ceased? When top

From the Experts ...
Life With Consultants: First, Prepare for the End
by Elaine Patterson, Senior Human Resources Consultant,
Unocal Corporation

How will these changes work after Consultant X leaves? Too often, someone raises that question one week before a consultant's contract is due to end, often at the final debriefing session. By then, it's too late to cram all the learning in, and the question leads to complaints about the thousands of dollars walking out the door.

We at Unocal Corporation are trying to do a better job of asking "What will happen when the consultant leaves?" beginning with the first meeting with the consultant, even before requests for proposals. Through this process, we are gaining insight into the consultants' view of how they want to work with us (vs. what they want to do *for* us). This is helping both parties think about moving from a consulting relationship to a partner relationship.

Thinking about the end of a project at the beginning has affected the outcomes on several projects. As just one example, when we engaged a global consulting firm to implement a job evaluation methodology, it was critical to identify the internal staff who would be responsible for learning the methodology and maintaining its credibility after the consultant's involvement was over. This allowed us to take greater ownership of the results (don't blame the consultant!) and not depend on external resources indefinitely.

When we contracted for a change-management consultant to work with a business unit, we explained to everyone involved that the human resources (HR) manager would be partnered with that consultant to perform all aspects of the work. This allowed us to systematically transfer change-management and internal consulting skills to the HR manager during the course of the project. There was no mad dash to transfer knowledge at the end. The results were a better business strategy for the unit (the overt outcome of the engagement) and an extraordinary development opportunity for the HR manager.

By discussing "What happens when the consultant leaves?" at the beginning of a project, the conversation shifts from "How much do we have to spend to have this work done?" to "How much do we need to invest to learn to do this work better and improve our own capability?"

management approved the plan for the redesign of the production process? When the workers in the hubcaps division began their training on the new equipment? When the workers completed their training? When the new production process was fully operational? When it was evident that output in the hubcaps division had increased appreciably and that the change in the production system had led to the desired results?

As you can see, determining when your involvement should end is not always easy. Frequently, clients seek the consultant's involvement in those parts of a project in which the client organization does not have expertise. However, the client may want internal staff to handle those parts of the project in which expertise is available.

Deciding just where and when you can add the most value is sometimes a difficult decision, and sometimes this decision will change as your involvement in the project increases. On the one hand, you don't want to bail out of a project before all the work is completed. On the other hand, you don't want to remain involved if you are no longer performing work covered under your contract. It is not uncommon for a client to suggest amending a contract to cover additional work. At Willis, for example, the initial contract may have specified that your work was finished once the employees were trained in how to use the new equipment. However, what if some unexpected problems arose? In that case, you and the client might have agreed that you should stay on for an indefinite period to ensure that the unit was operating efficiently and that all questions and concerns had been addressed.

Regardless of when your contractual obligations are over, you need to ensure that there is a smooth transition after you leave. You should work directly with the people in the organization who will be responsible for completing any work that remains after your departure. Most probably, the responsibility for completing the project will rest with the project coordinator or project manager at the client organization. If there is no one who fulfills that role, someone should be appointed. This person will be responsible for making sure that all the remaining tasks are completed.

You, the project manager, and perhaps the client should then develop a brief project plan that answers the following questions:

* What are the tasks or activities that remain to be done?
* Who will be responsible for completing each task?
* What are the start and completion dates for each task?
* What resources and information are needed to complete these tasks?

Addressing these questions is especially critical for large projects. A major disconnect can cause a project that was going along smoothly to collapse; even a minor disconnect after you leave can cause major problems. The key is to identify when your work ends and another person's begins. The same principles apply whether the other person is an external consultant or an internal employee. Again, the more planning that can be done early on, the better defined everyone's roles will be, resulting in fewer conflicts and misunderstandings between you and the client.

FINAL REPORTS

Some consultants regularly submit final reports that summarize the work they have done as well as the outcomes the project has produced. Other consultants make a practice of never delivering final reports unless clients absolutely insist on receiving them.

You should discuss with the client whether you will be expected to write a final report in your initial contract discussions with the client. Clarifying expectations surrounding this question, as in every area, will result in fewer unpleasant surprises.

Many clients want no more than a short memo indicating that the project has been completed. This provides them with a written record attesting to this fact. Other clients want longer, more formal documents that outline what you were contracted to do, the activities that have been completed, and the outcomes that have been obtained. Regardless of the format, the specifications for this report should be agreed on, including length and content, during contract discussions. You also will need to be sure to estimate the time required to write the report when estimating your fees and make sure that you are receiving payment for time spent preparing the document.

Most clients think that final reports are necessary and valuable. Organizations routinely spend considerable money, often millions, on consulting projects. Superiors within the organization want proof that serious work has been done and, more important, that the work produced the outcomes that were promised. Final reports provide justification that a project was worth the time and cost that went into it.

Although some consultants may view writing a final report as an unwanted, unpleasant task, a better way to approach it is as a good marketing opportunity. In preparing a final report, you have a chance to document the work you have accomplished. You may also want to highlight the quality of the work, that it was completed on time and under budget (assuming it was), as well as some of the unexpected benefits for the client.

Moreover, the report provides you with an opportunity to suggest future projects in which you might play a major role. Although this is clearly a means of soliciting further business, clients are usually appreciative of the expert advice and ideas on how you might help in furthering improve the company.

Even if the client does not expect a final report, it's good practice to include something in writing with your final invoice. It doesn't have to be more than a short note describing the project and indicating that the work, as stipulated in the contract, has been completed. This will remind the client what services are covered under the final invoice. It is also a good idea to add a few words about how much you appreciated working with the client and that you would welcome the chance to work with the client again.

The format and length of final reports vary considerably, but they usually include the following elements:

- *Salutation/title page:* Who the report is for, who the report is from, the date, and a title that clearly represents the contents.
- *Purpose:* A brief description of what topics are covered.
- *Overview of the project:* Why was the project initiated? Who was the principal sponsor? What outcomes were expected? What units and managers were involved? What was the timeline? What methods were used?
- *Outline of major activities:* What were the major activities, and what were the start and completion dates?
- *General results:* What results did the project produce, and how are these results linked to the outcomes that were expected? Whenever possible, results should be quantifiable, such as cost savings and increased sales.
- *Discussion:* What were the successes and limitations of the project?
- *Next steps:* Suggestions for additional projects that would build on the current project; in a multiplant company, for instance, the consultant might suggest expanding the project to other plants. The consultant may also want to suggest new projects aimed at increasing the effectiveness of the organization. Included should be some indication of the consultant's willingness and competency to take on these projects.

In addition to these components, longer reports often include an executive summary, right after the salutation/title page.

CLIENT–CONSULTANT DEBRIEFING

Many consultants like to arrange a final debriefing with the client. The purpose of this meeting is to review what went on during the project and to discuss ways the process could be improved in the future. Because some clients may not be familiar with such meetings and may have some reservations about participating, you should be sure to explain the goals and the overall agenda to the client beforehand.

The debriefing enables the client to provide you with feedback on the project, including such matters as how you conducted yourself. In addition, it signals that you want to improve the effectiveness of the projects you conduct and that you care about strengthening the client–consultant relationship.

The agenda of the meeting might look something like the following:

- Review of the purpose of the meeting, the agenda, and the amount of time set aside for each item.
- Brief review of the purpose, goals, major events, and outcomes of the project.

- The client's evaluation of the project. Did the project meet the client's expectations? What worked well, and what didn't, and why? How might a similar project be handled more effectively in the future?
- The consultant's evaluation of the project. This presentation should be prepared in advance and should demonstrate that you have spent considerable time thinking about the project. The focus should be on both those parts of the project that went well and those that were less effective. The presentation should end with a description of what you learned from working on the project and ways to be more effective when working on future projects for this client.
- The client's evaluation of the consultant's role (or of the role of the consulting firm). In what ways were you or the firm effective, and how could you have been more effective?

Sometimes consultants also discuss their perception of the client's role in the project, including areas in which the client was particularly helpful or effective and areas in which the client could be more helpful in the future. The goal here should be to assist the client in becoming more effective in whatever role he or she plays. Some clients ask for such feedback. Others may be unaccustomed to having consultants comment on their personal effectiveness and not want any feedback at all. Thus, comment on the client's effectiveness only if you think the client would welcome and accept it. However, under no circumstances should you appear to be blaming the client for things that did not work well.

One fairly nonthreatening way to introduce your feedback is to ask the client: "What did you personally learn from the project that could be applied to future projects? What could you have done that would have improved the project or helped it run more smoothly?" Questions of this type are likely to encourage the client to reflect on his or her involvement in the project and to become more receptive to the idea of receiving feedback as well as giving it.

If appropriate, before the debriefing is over, ask the client about the next steps in the project or about other projects the client sees in the future. If the client mentions a project in which you might want to get involved, make your interest clear and ask whether you and the client might be able to set up a meeting to discuss that project in more detail. Even if the client does not mention a specific project in which you or your firm might become involved, make it clear that you are interested in working with the company again in the future.

Finally, some consultants use debriefing meetings as opportunities to explore ways the client might be able to assist the consultant in soliciting business. Several options are possible here. Some consultants ask the client if they may use them as a reference. Some consultants also ask clients for the names of business contacts, such as other managers in their organization, who might be interested in their services. As a further step, some consultants ask the client for a letter of introduction or a recommendation to give to potential clients.

Although many consultants feel uncomfortable asking clients for referrals or recommendations, one research study found that the marketing strategy that most differentiated successful consultants from less successful consultants was that the former made considerably more use of referrals clients had given them. So, whether you are uncomfortable doing it or not, asking for referrals is very effective in generating future business.

The debriefing should end with your thanking the client for allowing you to work together. You should also mention, briefly but sincerely, that you hope you and the client can work together again. We strongly recommend that you also send a follow-up letter thanking the client for participating in a profitable meeting, thanking the client again for choosing you to assist on the project, and reiterating your desire to work with the client again in the future.

CELEBRATE!

The successful completion of a project is worthy of a celebration. If the project has been a success, a lot of people have worked hard and contributed extensive effort. Often, the project team will meet for lunch or dinner. There may be (usually humorous) speeches, and sometimes there are humorous awards. The event is designed to be fun and to thank everyone for a job well done.

A more reserved way to say thank you and celebrate is for you and the client to go out to dinner alone or with your spouses/partners. These events are usually more personal and formal than a lunch or dinner with the whole team.

Whether you have an informal lunch, a formal dinner, or some other celebration, the idea is to end the project on a positive, upbeat note. People appreciate and remember celebrations, and they reinforce the perception that the project has been a success.

KEEPING IN CONTACT

We strongly encourage you to see the ending of a project as setting the stage for working on another project for the same client. Most consultants make their livings from repeat business. However, repeat business does not happen automatically. You'll want to be sure to take special care to ensure that the client remains aware that you are both able and willing to work on other projects. As a general rule, organizations do not want to search for a new vendor every time they need a consultant's services. They would much prefer to establish long-term relationships with a few consultants, particularly those whom the client perceives are capable and trustworthy and who offer useful services at a reasonable price. In other words, the probability of obtaining repeat business is good, but you have to work to earn it.

Keeping in touch with current and former clients is critical if you are hoping for repeat business. Some large consulting firms publish monthly or bimonthly magazines that focus on issues of particular interest to organizations likely to use their services. Other firms distribute newsletters that contain shorter articles, perhaps a review of a new business book, as well as information on the projects in which the firm is currently involved.

Another low-cost way to keep in touch is to send clients reprints of articles that relate to a problem or topic in which they are likely to be interested, maybe something from the *Harvard Business Review* or the *Wall Street Journal* or a trade magazine in the client's area. Ideally, these articles should offer ideas of ways clients can improve their businesses. Many consultants occasionally phone or e-mail clients to find out how they're doing as well as to find out about projects they might be considering. Some consultants also visit former clients or invite them out for lunch periodically. One consultant sends his clients cards on their birthdays. Many send cards at the beginning of the year, perhaps with a small gift, such as a date book with the consultant's business name on it, or a subscription to a business magazine.

Regardless of the method you use to keep in touch, it should be grounded in a well-defined marketing strategy. Finding new or repeat business should be not a random event but based on a well-thought-out approach that has been demonstrated to produce repeat business. For example, one consultant regularly calls six former clients each week just to touch base. He claims that he produces sufficient business to keep him busy. Another consultant exerts most of her marketing energy at conventions and conferences attended by former and potential clients. She has found that the contacts she makes at these conventions generate her best business. Obtaining repeat business is hard work; however, the work is likely to pay much higher dividends if your marketing plan is a solid one.

SUMMARY

This chapter has focused on the importance of ending a project strategically and formally. We have provided you with many ideas for ending projects effectively. As with the other chapters in the book, we have listed next several success factors for ending projects effectively and on a positive note. We hope that learning these and the other success factors in this book will help you to become a truly effective consultant.

KEY SUCCESS FACTORS FOR ENDING A PROJECT

- Agree at the beginning of the project what activities will be conducted in the final stage (e.g., debriefing, writing a final report, quantifiable activities).
- Make sure that whatever transitions need to take place occur smoothly.
- Celebrate the completion of the project.
- Hold a final debriefing with the client with the goal of making the next project even more successful.
- Take advantage of the final stage of the project to establish a long-term relationship with the client.
- Seek further business from the client, or ask the client's assistance in finding future business.
- Keep in touch with the client; the chance of being rehired will be much higher.

CHAPTER
10

Some Final Thoughts: The Basic Principles of Effective Consulting

Are there basic principles of effective consulting, a philosophy by which effective consultants live? In the process of collecting data to write this book, we asked 100 successful consultants to think back over their careers and tell us the four or five most effective consulting principles that contributed to their success. We weren't interested in specific skills or techniques as previously outlined in this book; instead, we wanted to hear their general philosophy (or guidelines) about being an effective consultant. As you might expect, the question elicited a variety of responses. However, as often happens in such questioning, everyone agreed on five important points.

REMEMBER THE BASICS

The first principle that all the consultants mentioned is best introduced with an analogous story. Imagine for a moment that you're watching a tennis tournament. Brayden, a nationally ranked player, is quickly losing his big lead. He isn't serving as well as he usually does, and his returns aren't as strong as in the past. He's making a lot of errors and can't understand why. He begins to think he needs a new tennis racquet, a new strategy, or maybe he should change his grip. Before long, he has nearly lost the match. Just in time, he's reminded of his coach's mantra—"If you ever get into trouble, go back to the basics; more often than not, it's just the basics that will pull you out of trouble." Brayden did just that and wins the tournament!

When Brayden goes to the first meeting with his coach after the match, his coach offers some solid advice: "For awhile, Brayden, you forgot the basics. Remember, you need to keep your eye on the ball, to follow through, and to keep your feet moving. Unless you've laid that groundwork, and stick with it, nothing you do beyond that will be effective."

"I know," Brayden says. "I almost lost it. I just couldn't quit making errors. I was feeling overwhelmed by the competition and lost my focus. I started to think that I needed a new raquet, or to change my grip, or to learn a new technique. I just kept thinking there's got to be something major that's wrong with my game. But then, I remembered your mantra: 'When you're in trouble, keep it simple and just remember the basics!'"

Later, Brayden and his coach watch a video of the match and, just as they predicted, Brayden did take his eye off the ball, he didn't follow through on his strokes, and he was a bit flat-footed. He nearly lost an important match because he lost sight of the basics.

The same is true of consulting—and, for that matter, just about everything in life. This is exactly what we heard from the successful consultants we interviewed: "Never lose sight of the basics." They noted that often when they faltered in a consulting project it was because they did just that—lost sight of the basics. They didn't clarify the client's expectations, or they put together the contract too hurriedly, or they didn't have everybody on board with their project strategy before they started implementing action. Perhaps they were thinking too much about what would benefit them, instead of their client. They didn't take time to build the client's trust and confidence. And, in many cases, the result of this failure to stick to the basics was a consulting project that went poorly.

This book is all about the basics of consulting. Every chapter is devoted to one or more of the steps in executing a project. Throughout, we have pointed out what consultants need to do to successfully accomplish each step. Among the basics we have emphasized is the need to clarify expectations, to write a strong initial proposal, to prepare thoroughly for every meeting, to diagnose the problem comprehensively, and to commit the client to action. Remembering these basics will keep you on target and help make you a successful consultant.

ESTABLISH SOLID RELATIONSHIPS

Of the consultants we interviewed, all of them mentioned that another principle to success is to build solid, trusted relationships. One consultant said "It's *all* about relationships." As should be clear from the cases and examples in this book, for a project to succeed, there must be trust between the consultant and the client, just as there must in any successful relationship. Not surprisingly, before a client will want you to work on any of the pieces of a project, there will have to be a great deal of trust between you and the client. Without trust, the relationship—and, therefore, your work as a consultant—cannot go forward. After all, the client is putting an organization's future in your hands. The client can do this only if there is a great deal of trust in both your abilities and your motives. In our "From the Experts ..." section in this last chapter, Raj Tatta, a partner at PricewaterhouseCoopers, effectively explains the importance of developing strong relationships with clients. Tatta claims that consultants cannot be truly successful without caring for their clients and building strong and lasting relationships. Consistent with our next principle for success, Tatta also notes there is nothing more important than serving your client.

FOCUS ON HELPING THE CLIENT

As one successful consultant reminded us, "Never, ever, forget that you are here to serve the client and to help the client move the organization to a higher level of effectiveness." This summarizes the next success guideline. Consulting is a service or helping profession. The client's interests must always come first. It is not about completing a contract or selling the client a product but rather it is about moving the organization to a higher level of effectiveness.

Some people have likened the relationship between consultant and client to that of a medical doctor and patient. The patient goes to the doctor hoping to become healthier, either by correcting a problem or improving his or her lifestyle. The doctor diagnoses the problem and recommends a treatment strategy until the patient achieves his or her objectives and is healthier. In the process, rediagnosis may be necessary, to clarify that the doctor has the diagnosis right or to identify a different diagnosis. The doctor may also need to make adjustments in treatment, even after it's begun. Regardless, throughout the process, the doctor is expected to remain committed to the patient and to improving the patient's health.

Several of the consultants we interviewed mentioned that a similar relationship exists between consultants and their clients. There should be no question that you are 100% in the client's corner. Your commitment is to help the organization improve. And if the tasks agreed on in the contract aren't delivering the expected outcomes, then you need to think things through from the client's perspective and redesign the intervention (and the contract). The client's interests must always come before your own. In the long term, this approach will also best serve your interests, because commitment and trust are also the keys to repeat business.

ALWAYS PLAY IT STRAIGHT

Another key principle identified by the successful consultants we interviewed was related to ethical behavior. "Play it straight," "Keep above

From the Experts ...
**Building Strong Consultant–Client Relationships at
PricewaterhouseCoopers
by Raj Tatta, Partner, PricewaterhouseCoopers**

An important truism in business is that people only buy from people they like and trust. This is the case whether they're buying products or services. This is particularly true if the product or service does not have a significant differentiator, in either quality or price. In other words, in any service profession, such as consulting, relationship skills are critical to success.

Most important, your clients need to like you and trust you. This takes time and concerted effort. Customers cannot like you if they don't have a chance to get to know you. Therefore, you have to constantly look for ways to let your clients get to know you better. They have to see you in action—as a human being and as a professional. They have to conclude that you (and your organization) are the kind they want to do business with. You need to find out their interests and hobbies, the organizations they belong to, and so on, and show interest in them as human beings.

The second aspect of the adage above is trust. Developing trust is even more difficult than getting clients to like you. It has been my experience that, for a relationship with a client to be successful, the client has to first trust you as a human being—your values, your integrity, and so forth. They also have to trust you as a professional. But, while fully recognizing that you're a businessperson intent on making money, the relationship with the client has to come before reaping immediate financial gains. This means that you must deliver on time as promised and act in your clients' interests each and every time. Instead of a supplier or a vendor, you have to become a trusted business adviser.

Nothing is more important than serving your client. At Pricewaterhouse-Coopers, we call it obsession with client service. The fact is that the vast majority of services you offer can't be distinguished from those of your competitors'. You can, however, achieve differentiation by adding value. Make sure that your client understands and appreciates the value you have added. This reaffirms the client's selection of you both in his or her eyes and in the eyes of the entire client organization.

Finally, try to have close personal relationships with your client. Without personal relationships, your clients won't discuss their business plans or their problems/issues, thereby denying you the opportunity to be of service.

Good relationships with clients often lead to friendships. We all know that we go the extra mile for friends, and our friends do the same for us. As important, we have more fun working with our friends. Therefore, when relationships with clients are based on friendship and engender a spirit of partnership, the resulting synergy creates the greatest value to both the buying and the selling organizations.

board," and "Always take the high road" were common themes. We're reminded of the devastating experience of Arthur Anderson, who got "sucked into" a client scheme and ultimately undertook illegal behaviors that nearly brought down the whole organization. The consultants we spoke with (fortunately) noted they rarely faced unethical situations. Their caution to students or new consultants was that if something smells fishy in the entry stage of the project, put up your guard, and never be afraid to turn down a consulting project that doesn't feel right from the beginning—most times, the situation doesn't get better over time but only gets worse.

These consultants noted that it is not worth the risk to you or your reputation to undertake unethical behaviors. It will not help the client in the long run, and it will not help your career. Probably the best help you can be to the client in questionable situations is to assist them in taking the high road and avoiding anything that smacks of unethical behavior. If the client insists on going ahead, and you are uncomfortable with the decisions, then it is time to leave the project.

There are several professional consulting associations that have established codes of conduct that apply to the consulting profession (e.g., the Institute of Management Consulting). If you ever have questions regarding the ethics of either your behavior or the client's behavior, these codes provide a valuable resource to help answer your questions.

ENJOY THE WORK!

"Have fun!" "Enjoy your work!" "Don't take yourself too seriously!" We heard this advice frequently from the consultants we interviewed. Successful consultants enjoy what they do, and their enjoyment affects the people with whom they work. Everyone feels more energetic and eager to get things done when the people involved in a project are upbeat and positive. Maintaining a positive, cheerful demeanor will reap rewards in the long run, too. Wouldn't you rather work with someone again with whom you had fun?

The consultants we spoke to also were quick to point out the personal rewards of consulting. As an effective consultant, you have the potential to positively affect the culture of a work unit or division by helping the people you're working with recognize the benefits they'll gain by making changes. You also have the opportunity to help them succeed as they implement changes. Helping others in this way can be a lot of fun—and a cause for celebrating and feeling a great sense of pride. You have truly affected the course of other people's work lives, as well, perhaps, of an organization's earnings. And, as all our consultants hastened to add, you can get paid handsomely for providing this service.

FINAL THOUGHTS

Consulting is a great profession. You're likely to meet great people, some of whom may become lifelong friends.

You'll get to work on a variety of projects and studies. No two consulting projects are alike. Each project provides new challenges and approaches and enables you to use your creativity. The variety of the work and the people you'll meet makes the consulting business exciting and fun.

We sincerely hope you have gained a lot of practical advice from reading this book. Equally important, however, we hope you have come to recognize the impact you can have as a consultant on individuals and organizations. Consultants can significantly enhance the work lives of departments, divisions, and entire organizations. When this happens, not only is a product or service improved but so too are the lives of individual workers. What can be more rewarding than that!

Good luck! We wish you the best of success and enjoyment in this exciting profession.

FIVE KEY BASIC SUCCESS PRINCIPLES
OF EFFECTIVE CONSULTING

1. Remember the basics.
2. Establish solid relationships.
3. Focus on helping the client.
4. Always play it straight.
5. Enjoy the work.

Some Further Reading

For readers who are serious about being effective consultants, the learning process is never ending. Consulting is about change, about new techniques and approaches, which means that consulting is like any other business: One cannot succeed with yesterday's skills or by resting on yesterday's laurels. Instead, you must continually look for ways to improve your skills and knowledge. Fortunately, a variety of resources are available to help you do this. We have found the ones listed in this section to be particularly helpful.

Starting a Consulting Practice

The following two books are designed for those interested in starting a consulting practice from scratch. They offer very basic advice on getting started.

Biech, E. (2001). *The consultant's quick start guide: An action plan for your first year in business.* San Francisco: Pfeiffer.

Weiss, A. (2003). *Getting started in consulting* (2nd ed.). New York: Wiley.

Growing the Practice

For those looking to grow your business, try the following:

Biech, E. (2003). *Marketing your consulting services.* San Francisco: Pfeiffer.

Weiss, A. (2002). *Million dollar consulting: The professional's guide to growing a practice.* New York: McGraw-Hill.

Proposals and Contracts

One of the areas that consultants find difficult is writing proposals and contracts. The following are some helpful sources.

Fishman, S. (2004). *Consulting and independent contractor agreements*. Berkeley, CA: Nolo.

Holtz, H. (1997). *Complete guide to consulting contracts* (2nd ed.). Chicago: Upstart.

Holtz, H. (1998). *The consultant's guide to proposal writing* (3rd ed.). New York: Wiley.

Weiss, A. (2003). *How to write a proposal that is accepted every time* (2nd ed.). New York: Kennedy Information.

Consulting Process

In this book we have outlined the step-by-step process of helping a client, beginning with the initial contact and ending with the successful completion of the work. The following two books complement the approach taken here.

Block, P. (1999). *Flawless consulting: A guide to getting your expertise used*. San Francisco: Pfeiffer.

Weiss, A. (2002). *Process consulting: How to launch, implement, and conclude successful consulting projects*. San Francisco: Pfeiffer.

Strategies of the Major Firms

One of the differences among consultants is whether they own their own business or work for a large consulting company, many of whom have several thousand consultants on staff. The major firms typically take on the big, expensive, long-term projects, whereas independent consultants usually become involved in smaller, often short-term projects. The two books listed next convey some of the culture of the major firms, which is usually quite different than that of the smaller companies. Biswas and Twitchell's book contains (among other information) short statements about the approaches used by about 15 or 20 of the major firms. The second book, by Rasiel, is about McKinsey, the premier firm focusing on organizational strategy. The book provides a nice explanation of the approach and techniques used by McKinsey, which is a large firm specializing in organizational strategy.

Biswas, S. & Twitchell, D. (2001). *Management consulting: A complete guide to the industry* (2nd ed.). New York: Wiley.

Rasiel, E. M. (1999). *The McKinsey way.* New York: McGraw-Hill.

Keeping Current

When consultants talk about "keeping current," they usually are referring to two related ideas. The first suggests being up to date on the latest business ideas and trends—in leadership development, e-commerce, globalization, or governance. To keep current on these issues, we recommend reading the *Harvard Business Review,* the *Wall Street Journal,* or a similar publication that covers the latest ideas being discussed in the world of business.

Another meaning of the term *current* is the latest in techniques being used in a specific area of business, such as accounting, information technology, quality, or the like. For information on these areas, we recommend the associations for specialists in these areas as well as the professional journals these associations publish. Associations are the best source—often, the only source—for learning about the latest developments in accounting, information technology, and so forth.

Finally, a good source on the latest developments in some 20 specialty areas of management consulting (although this may be more than you really want to know) is:

Greiner, L., & Poulfelt, F. (2004). *Handbook of management consulting: The contemporary consultant, insights from the world experts.* Mason, OH: South-Western.

Index

Note: *f* indicate figure, *t* indicates table.